ANY BITCH

CAN PARTY!

A

COOKBOOK

FOR ALL YOUR

ENTERTAINING

Entertaining is a delightful way to bring friends, acquaintances and family together. It rewards the soul and spirit and creates life long relationships. By inviting guests to your home, they know their presence is important to you! Hospitality is a definite way to show your caring and appreciation for others.

With recipes in this book you will be able to mix and match to your personal lifestyle and tastes. I have tried to give you choices in preparing your party. One of the secrets to having a great party is to be able to prepare in advance of the party day. Most of these recipes allow you to do this!

From a personal perspective, cooking a regular meal never seemed very rewarding considering the time it took to plan and prepare and then devoured in five minutes. But entertaining brings such pleasure to me because it brings joy to those that are invited to get away from the daily pressures of life and all its responsibilities.

Through the years of raising a family, owning a motel and restaurant and being blessed with many friends and family, who are excellent cooks, these recipes have evolved. Thanks to the many friends who have allowed me to use their recipes in this book. THANKS!

LET'S PARTY
Jackie McClure

I WOULD LIKE TO SAY A

SPECIAL " THANK YOU" TO

TWO GREAT FRIENDS,

CAROL ADAMS

AND

CERETHA ROSE,

FOR ALL THEIR HELP.

Table of Contents

Index

NEW YEARS DAY CELEBRATION

VIRGIN BLOODY MARYS

BLOODY MARYS

JALAPENO EGGS

SPINACH DIP

BLACK EYED PEAS WITH SAUSAGE

SOUR CREAM CORN MUFFINS

PRALINE COOKIES

GRAND MARNIER SAUCE FOR FRUIT

ALL GLORY COMES FROM
DARING TO BEGIN.

1

VIRGIN MARYS

7 oz. tomato juice
½ oz. lemon juice
Salt and pepper to taste
1/8 tsp. celery seed

3 dashes Worcestershire sauce
1 dash Tabasco sauce
1 stick of celery
1 lime wedge

Combine all the ingredients, except the stick of celery and lime wedge. Fill a highball glass with ice and pour mixture over the ice. Garnish with the celery and lime. Serves 1.

BLOODY MARYS

2-10 oz. cans Snap-E-Tom
¾ C. vodka

3 C. tomato juice
Celery sticks, with tops

Freeze the Snap-E-Tom in ice trays overnight. Mix tomato juice and vodka in a pitcher. Place 3 to 4 Snap-E-Tom ice cubes in a glass and pour tomato juice mixture over them. Add the celery stick. Makes 1 qt.

JALAPENO EGGS

Fort Stockton, TX. New Years Dance

3 dz. hard-boiled eggs, peeled
2 onions, sliced

White vinegar
1 large bottle sliced jalapenos, save the juice

Mix the same amount of vinegar and jalapeno juice together in a saucepan. Bring to a boil. In a wide mouth gallon jar, layer eggs, onions and jalapenos. Pour the vinegar mixture over the eggs. If you need more liquid, use vinegar. Refrigerate for 2 weeks.

SPINACH DIP

1-10 oz. pkg. frozen chopped spinach
1 C. sour cream
1 C. mayonnaise

1 pkg. Knorr's vegetable soup mix
1 medium onion, chopped
1 small can water chestnuts, sliced

Thaw the frozen spinach and squeeze the water out. Do not cook the spinach.
Combine remaining ingredients and mix with the spinach. Chill.

BLACK EYED PEA AND SAUSAGE DISH

Fort Stockton, TX. New Years Dance

¼ lb. bacon, fried and crumbled
1 C. chopped celery
1 C. chopped green peppers
1 C. chopped onions
1 ring German sausage, sliced

1-14 oz. can peeled tomatoes
1 bag frozen black-eyed peas
2 jalapenos
½ tsp. sugar
garlic salt to taste

In a large pan, sauté the celery, green peppers and onions in the bacon grease.
Add the sausage, bacon, tomatoes, peas, jalapenos, sugar and garlic salt. Salt
and pepper. Add water to cover. Cook several hours on low. Serves 8.

SOUR CREAM CORN MUFFINS

1 C. self-rising yellow cornmeal mix
1 tsp. salt
1- 8 oz. carton sour cream

1 can cream-style corn
¼ C. vegetable oil
2 eggs, lightly beaten

Mix all the ingredients well. Spoon into a greased muffin pan, filling two-thirds full. Bake in a preheated 400 degrees F. oven for 25 minutes. Makes 12 muffins.

PRALINE COOKIES

¼ lb. pecan halves
20 single honey graham crackers

1 C. butter
2 C. firmly packed brown sugar

Place pecan halves in rows on top on the crackers. Place on an ungreased cookie sheet. In an iron skillet cook butter and sugar over medium heat until melted together, stirring constantly. Remove from heat, and spoon mixture over each graham cracker. Bake in a preheated 300 degree F. oven for 10 minutes. Place on waxed paper to cool. Makes 20 cookies.

GRAND MARNIER SAUCE FOR FRUIT

Carol Adams, Fort Stockton, TX.

4 egg yolks
¾ C. sugar
1 tsp. lemon juice
Dash of salt

2 T. flour
¾ C. Grand Marnier
1 pt. whipping cream

Beat egg yolks, and place in a double boiler. Stir in sugar, lemon juice and salt. Make paste of flour and small amount of the Grand Marnier. Mix well. Add remaining Grand Marnier. Add to eggs stirring constantly until thick. Cool. Whip cream and fold into mixture. Chill. Spoon over the fruit of your choose.

NOTES

SUPER BOWL PARTY

CRANBERRY PINEAPPLE PUNCH

CHAMPAGNE FIZZ

HOT WINGS   SPICY CLAM DIP

SEAFOOD GUMBO

OLD-FASHION CORN BREAD

RUM CAKE

"WINNING CAN BE DEFINED AS THE SCIENCE
OF BEING TOTALLY PREPARED."
GEORGE ALLEN

CRANBERRY PINEAPPLE PUNCH

2-1 qt. cranberry juice cocktail, chilled
1-1 qt. can unsweetened pineapple juice, chilled

2 C. ginger ale, chilled
2 C. seltzer water, chilled

In a large punch bowl combine all the ingredients. Add an ice block and serve.
Makes about 20 cups.

CHAMPAGNE FIZZ

1 fifth champagne
1-6 oz. can frozen lemonade
1 C. orange juice

6 oz. club soda
6 oz. vodka
2 C. ice cubes

Place all the ingredients in a blender, except champagne. Pour 1 oz. champagne
in each glass and fill with blender mixture. Serves 6 to 8.

SPICY CLAM DIP WITH RAW VEGETABLES

1-15 oz. can New England clam chowder
1 ½ -8 oz. pkg. cream cheese, softened

2 T. minced onion
2 T. prepared horseradish
2 T. Worcestershire sauce

Place all the ingredients in a blender and blend till smooth. Serve with raw
vegetables. Makes 4 cups.

HOT WINGS

12 chicken wings
1 C. butter, melted
Tabasco sauce to taste

½ tsp. salt
½ tsp. pepper

Cut the tips off the wings. Mix the butter, Tabasco, salt and pepper in a large bowl. Coat the wings with mixture. Deep fry at 350 degrees F. for 12 minutes.

SEAFOOD GUMBO

6 T. oil
2 lbs. okra, thinly sliced
1 T. flour
2 C. onions, finely chopped
½ C. celery, finely chopped
½ C. green pepper, finely chopped
2 cloves garlic, pressed
1-16 oz. can tomato paste
2 bay leaves
¼ tsp. thyme
1 T. salt
½ tsp. Tabasco

½ tsp. cayenne pepper
½ tsp. pepper
½ tsp. Cajun seasoning
1 T. Worcestershire
1-16 oz. can chopped tomatoes
1 can Rotel green chilies
8 C. water
4 lbs. raw shrimp, peeled and deveined
1 lb. crabmeat
2 dz. oysters in their liquid
2 T. parsley, chopped
5 C. steamed rice

In a large iron skillet, heat 4 tablespoons of oil and add the okra. Cook over medium heat, stirring often, 40 to 50 minutes. In a large soup pot, pour 2 tablespoons oil and blend the flour until roux is dark brown. Add the onion and celery and cook until tender. Add the green pepper, tomato paste, onion and garlic. Cook 3 more minutes. Stir in the bay leaves, thyme, salt, Tabasco, cayenne pepper, pepper, Cajun seasoning and Worcestershire. Add the tomatoes and green chilies and stir until smooth. Add the cooked okra. Gradually stir in the water. Add the shrimp and cover. Simmer over low heat for 30 minutes. Add the crabmeat and simmer 30 minutes. Add the oysters and the liquid and parsley and cook for 10 minutes. Serve over the rice. Serves 10.

OLD-FASHION CORN BREAD

¼ C. butter
1 C. yellow cornmeal
1 C. flour
1 T. baking powder
¼ tsp. baking soda

½ tsp. salt
2 T. sugar
1 ¼ C. buttermilk
1 egg, beaten
¼ C. corn oil

In an 8-inch iron skillet, melt the butter. In a bowl, mix the next 6 ingredients. Add the rest of the ingredients and mix well. Pour the batter into the skillet. Cook in a preheated 375 degrees F. oven for 25 to 30 minutes. Serves 6.

RUM CAKE

¼ lb. butter, softened
½ C. Cisco
2 C. sugar
4 eggs
3 C. flour
½ tsp. baking soda

½ tsp. baking powder
¼ tsp. salt
1 C. buttermilk
1 tsp. vanilla
1 tsp. rum flavoring

Cream butter, Cisco and sugar. Add the eggs one at time. In another bowl, add the dry ingredients and mix. Alternating with flour mixture and buttermilk add to the cream mixture. Add the flavoring and mix well. Pour into a greased bundt pan. Bake in a preheated 325 degrees F. oven for 1 hour. Pour glaze over the hot cake.

Glaze:

2 sticks butter
1 C. sugar

2 oz. rum

Melt the butter and sugar over low heat. Add the rum. Mix well.

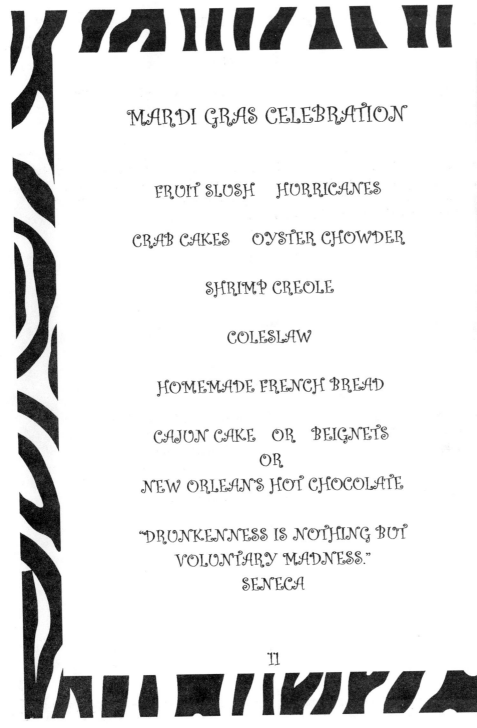

MARDI GRAS CELEBRATION

FRUIT SLUSH   HURRICANES

CRAB CAKES   OYSTER CHOWDER

SHRIMP CREOLE

COLESLAW

HOMEMADE FRENCH BREAD

CAJUN CAKE   OR   BEIGNETS
OR
NEW ORLEAN'S HOT CHOCOLATE

"DRUNKENNESS IS NOTHING BUT
VOLUNTARY MADNESS."
SENECA

11

FRUIT SLUSH

2 C. orange juice

2 bananas

1 C. sugar

#2 can crushed pineapple

2 lemons, juiced

2 C. ginger ale

Make the orange juice as to the can directions. Mash the bananas and blend in the sugar thoroughly. Add all the rest of the ingredients and blend well. Pour in a pyrex dish and freeze. Take out of the freezer and let stand for an hour. It needs to be in a slushy state. Serves 10 to 12.

HURRICANES

4 oz. dark rum

4 oz. light rum

2 oz. Galliano

8 oz. passion fruit syrup

2 oz. orange juice

4 T. lime juice

4 T. pineapple juice

Place in a pitcher and mix. Pour over glasses of ice. Serves 4.

CRAB CAKES

1 lb. crabmeat
¼ C. green pepper, finely chopped
¼ C. onion, finely chopped
¼ C. miracle whip
1 egg, beaten
1 C. bread crumbs, unseasoned

1 T. Old Bay seasoning
1 T. parsley flakes
½ tsp. dry mustard
½ tsp. salt
¼ tsp. pepper
½ tsp. Worcestershire sauce

Mix altogether and form into patties. Fry in butter or bake in a preheated 375 degrees F. oven for 20 minutes. Makes 6 to 8.

OYSTER CHOWDER

1 lb. shucked oysters in liquid
¼ lb. bacon, finely chopped
1 C. celery, thinly sliced
1 C. onion, diced
3 C. potatoes, peeled and diced
1 C. carrot, sliced

1 C. water
1 tsp. kosher salt
¼ tsp. pepper
¼ tsp. dried thyme
¼ C. butter
5 T. flour
4 C. half and half

Cut oysters in quarters. Save the liquid. In a large saucepot add the bacon, celery and onions. Cook until transparent. Remove the bacon, celery and onions from the pot and set aside. Place in the saucepot the potatoes, carrots, oyster liquid, water, salt, pepper and thyme. Bring to a boil, reduce heat and simmer until almost tender. Drain and remove all from the pan. Set aside. Add the butter to the pan and melt. Whisk in the flour and heat over medium heat until bubbly. Slowly whisk in the half and half. Add all the ingredients back in and mix well. Heat and stir without boiling. Serves 6 to 8.

SHRIMP CREOLE

Wanda Jones, Temple, TX.

¼ C. oleo
¼ C. flour
1 C. hot water
½ tsp. thyme
Dash cayenne pepper
1-8 oz. can tomato sauce
¼ C. chopped celery

½ C. chopped green onions
½ C. chopped parsley or 2 T. dried
4 garlic cloves, pressed or finely
   chopped
2 whole bay leaves
1 ½ lbs. raw shrimp, peeled
4 C. cooked rice

Prepare roux by heating oleo in a large skillet and blend in flour over medium heat. Stir constantly until dark brown. Be careful not to scorch. Add water gradually and cook until thick and smooth. Add remaining ingredients, except the shrimp and rice. Cook for 15 minutes. Add shrimp and cook for about 5 more minutes. Serve over rice. Serves 6 to 8.

COLESLAW

1 lb. cabbage, shredded
1 tsp. kosher salt
1 T. vinegar
1 T. sugar

½ tsp. Creole mustard
3 carrots, peeled and shredded
1 tsp. salt
½ tsp. pepper

Add the cabbage and kosher salt. Let stand 2 hours. Rinse and drain well. Dissolve the sugar in the vinegar. Stir in the mustard. Add the rest of the ingredients and mix well. Refrigerate. Serves 6.

14

HOMEMADE FRENCH BREAD

2 ½ C. warm water
1 pkg. yeast
2 T. sugar

1 tsp. salt
7 C. flour
3 egg whites, beaten

Dissolve yeast in warm water. Add the sugar and salt and mix well. Add the flour. Turn onto a floured surface and knead for 10 minutes. Place in a greased bowl, cover and let rise for 1½ hour. Punch bread down and knead 3 or 4 times. Divide into 4 parts. Shape each part into loaves and place them on a greased pan. Cut slashes on the tops of each loaf. Brush with the egg whites. Let rise 1 hour. Bake in a preheated 450 degrees F. oven for 30 minutes. Remove and cool.

CAJUN CAKE

Sue Walker, Lubbock, TX.

2 C. flour, all-purpose
2 C. sugar
2 eggs
1 ½ tsp. soda

1 C. flake coconut
1 C. pecans, chopped
1-20 oz. can crushed pineapple,
     with the juice
1 tsp. vanilla

Mix all the ingredients by hand. Pour into a greased 9x13-inch pan. Bake in a preheated 325 degrees F. oven for 45 minutes or until brown and firm to the touch. Ice the cake while still warm, not hot.

Icing:

1 C. powdered sugar
½ tsp. vanilla

1-8 oz. cream cheese, softened
½ stick oleo, softened

Mix well and ice the cake.

BEIGNETS

1 C. water	1 tsp. salt
1 C. milk	2 tsp. sugar
1 egg	Pinch of nutmeg
3 C. flour	6 C. vegetable oil
2 T. baking powder	Powdered sugar

Stir together the water, milk and egg in a bowl and mix well. Add the flour, baking powder, salt and sugar and mix well. Add the nutmeg. Mix. Heat the oil in a large deep pot. Drop the batter by spoonfuls into the hot oil and fry, turning 2 to 3 times. They should be golden brown. Drain on paper towel. Sprinkle with the powdered sugar. Makes about 2 dozen.

NEW ORLEAN'S HOT CHOCOLATE

2 ½ oz. unsweetened chocolate	2/3 C. sugar
½ C. water	½ C. whipping cream, whipped
½ tsp. salt	8 C. hot milk

Mix the chocolate and water over low heat until chocolate is melted. Add the salt and sugar. Bring to a boil and reduce heat. Simmer for 5 minutes. Cool. Fold in the whipping cream. You can store in the refrigerator until ready to serve. To serve, place 1 heaping tablespoon in each cup and fill with hot milk. Stir well. Makes 8 to 10 servings.

VALENTINE PARTY

CRANBERRY COOLER CRANBERRY RIESLING DRINK

COLD LOBSTER DIP

BEEF TENDERLOIN STUFFED WITH MUSHROOMS

SPINACH SALAD BOWL
WITH ORANGE BUTTERMILK DRESSING

PARSLEY POTATO BALLS

GREEN BEANS WITH HORSERADISH SAUCE

FLUFFY YEAST ROLLS

RED VELVET CAKE

"THE SUPREME HAPPINESS OF LIFE IS THE
CONVICTION THAT WE ARE LOVED."
VICTOR HUGO

17

CRANBERRY COOLER

4 oz. cranberry juice
2 oz. grape juice

2 oz. lemon-lime soda
1 lime wedge

Pour all the ingredients, except the lime wedge into a pitcher. Pour over ice and add the lime wedge. Serves 1.

CRANBERRY-RIESLING DRINK

2-12 oz. cans frozen cranberry juice,
   thawed and mixed according to can
4 C. Riesling, chilled

6 C. club soda, chilled
2 small lemons, thinly sliced

In a pitcher, stir together the cranberry juice and the wine. This can be mixed up to 6 hours ahead and chilled. When ready to serve, fill a large pitcher with ice cubes. Add the cranberry juice mixture and the club soda. Stir gently to mix. Serve in ice cube filled glasses, each garnished with a lemon slice. Makes 13 cups.

COLD LOBSTER DIP

1-8 oz. pkg. cream cheese, softened
4 T. butter, softened
1 T. lemon juice

1-7 oz. can lobster meat, drained
1 T. minced onion
1 T. + ½ tsp. prepared horseradish

Mix the cream cheese and butter until smooth. Add the rest of the ingredients. Mix well. Cover and refrigerate until ready to serve. This makes 16 servings.

BEEF TENDERLOIN STUFFED WITH MUSHROOMS

This recipe comes from a great friend, Carol Adams from Fort Stockton, TX. Thanks!

1 lb. fresh mushrooms, sliced
1C. chopped green onions
¼ C. chopped fresh parsley
1 (5 to 6 lb.) beef tenderloin
1 tsp. salt free herb and spice blend

½ C. soy sauce
1/3 C. dry sherry
2 T. honey
2 T. light brown sugar
1 T. vegetable oil
2 cloves garlic, minced

Coat a large, non-stick skillet with cooking spray. Place over medium heat until hot. Add mushrooms and green onions, sauté until tender. Drain. Stir in the parsley. Set aside. Trim excess fat from tenderloin. Cut tenderloin lengthwise from top to within ½ inch of bottom, leaving bottom connected. Sprinkle cut edges with the herb blend. Spoon mushroom mixture into opening of tenderloin; pull sides together. Tie securely with heavy string. Place tenderloin in a large, shallow dish. Set aside. Combine soy sauce and remaining ingredients. Pour over tenderloin. Cover and refrigerate 8 hours, basting occasionally with marinade. Drain tenderloin and place on a rack in a roasting pan. Insert meat thermometer, making sure it does not touch stuffing. Bake in a 425 degrees F. oven for 45 to 60 minutes or until meat thermometer registers 140 to 150 degrees. Transfer to a serving platter. Let stand 10 to 15 minutes before slicing. Serves 8 to 12.

SPINACH SALAD BOWL WITH ORANGE BUTTERMILK DRESSING

Dressing:

¼ C. orange juice
3 T. white wine vinegar
1 T. Dijon mustard
¼ C. mayonnaise

½ C. vegetable oil
½ C. buttermilk
2 tsp. grated orange zest
½ tsp. salt
¼ tsp. ground black pepper

Whisk together the orange juice, vinegar, mustard and mayonnaise. Gradually whisk in the oil and the buttermilk. Stir in orange zest, salt and pepper. This can be made one day ahead. Refrigerate.

Salad:

15 C. spinach leaves,
  stems removed and torn into
2 heads endive, cut up

3 oranges, peeled and cut up
1 C. pitted black olives
1 thinly slice peeled red onion

Place spinach and endive in a large salad bowl. Add the oranges. Sprinkle olives over oranges and scatter onion slices over the top of the salad. This can be made several hours ahead. Cover and refrigerate. Pour dressing over salad and toss just before serving. Serves 12 to 15.

PARSLEY POTATO BALLS

6 medium potatoes, peeled and cooked
2 T. butter or margarine
¼ C. dairy sour cream
½ tsp. salt
¼ tsp. pepper

1 egg
1 T. minced green onion
1 T. minced fresh parsley
2 T. butter, melted
¼ C. grated Parmesan cheese
Parsley sprigs

Mash the potatoes until smooth. Beat in the butter, sour cream, salt, pepper, egg, green onion and parsley. Shape into 12 (2-inch) balls. Refrigerate at least 2 hours. Preheat oven to 375 degrees F. Place potato balls in an ungreased 13"x9" baking pan. Brush with melted butter and sprinkle with Parmesan cheese. Bake 15 to 20 minutes or until lightly browned. Garnish with parsley sprigs. The potatoes can be made ahead and refrigerated up to 24 hours. Serves 6.

GREEN BEANS WITH HORSERADISH SAUCE

1 lb. fresh green beans
1 C. mayonnaise
2 hard-boiled eggs, chopped
2 T. horseradish
1 tsp. Worcestershire sauce
½ tsp. salt

1/8 tsp. pepper
½ tsp. garlic powder
½ tsp. celery salt
½ tsp. onion salt
1 ½ tsp. parsley flakes
Juice of 1 lemon

Steam green beans for 12 minutes. Blend the remaining ingredients. Set aside at room temperature. When ready to serve pour over hot beans. Serves 4. Beans are also good cold.

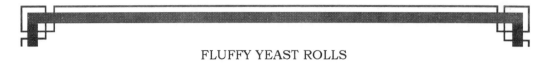

FLUFFY YEAST ROLLS

2 pkgs. yeast
½ C. warm water
1 C. milk, scalded
½ C. sugar
½ C. margarine

2 tsp. salt
5 ½ C. flour
3 eggs, beaten

Add yeast to ½ cup warm water and let stand for 10 minutes. Combine scalded milk, sugar, margarine and salt; cool to lukewarm. Stir in 2 cups flour and mix well. Add yeast mixture and eggs, mixing well. Add remaining flour to make a soft dough. Knead the dough for 10 minutes, until it becomes smooth and satiny. Put dough in oiled bowl, turning once to coast thoroughly. Cover with a damp towel and place in a warm spot. Allow to rise about 2 hours. Turn dough onto a lightly floured surface and roll into 1-inch balls and arrange on greased baking sheets. Cover with a damp towel and allow to rise until doubled, about 1 hour. Preheat oven to 375 degrees F. Bake 10 minutes, or until rolls are lightly browned. This makes 36 rolls.

RED VELVET CAKE

½ C. shortening
1 ½ C. sugar
2 eggs
1 tsp. vanilla
1 oz. red food color
3 T. cocoa

2 ½ C. flour
1 tsp. salt
1 C. buttermilk
1 T. vinegar
1 tsp. soda

Cream shortening, sugar, eggs and vanilla. Make a paste of food coloring and cocoa. Add to the first mixture. Mix flour and salt. Alternately add flour and buttermilk to the creamed mixture. Mix vinegar and soda in a cup. Add to the batter. Blend. Pour in 3 greased round cake pans. Bake in a preheated 350 degrees F. oven for 20-25 minutes. Let cool. Ice the cake.

Frosting

1 C. milk
3 T. flour
½ tsp. salt

1 C. sugar
1 C. shortening
2 tsp. vanilla

Combine milk, flour and salt in a saucepan. Cook until thick, stirring constantly. Let cool. Cream sugar and shortening thoroughly. Add the vanilla. Combine with cooled mixture. Beat well. Spread on the cooled cake.

NOTES

SAINT PATRICK'S DAY CELEBRATION

BLACKCURRANT PUNCH

GREEN BEER   EVERYBODY'S IRISH

SALMON MOUSSE

IRISH STEW

IRISH SODA BREAD

IRISH COFFEE

SHAMROCK COOKIES   FLAMING PEARS

"MAY YOUR BLESSINGS OUTNUMBER THE
SHAMROCKS THAT GROW, AND MAY
TROUBLE AVOID YOU WHEREVER YOU GO.

BLACKCURRANT PUNCH

6 C. water, boiling
8 T. blackcurrant jelly

2 lemons, juiced and save the rind
8 T. honey

In a 1-quart jar add the jelly, lemon juice, lemon rinds and honey. Pour the water into the jar. Stir well. Let stand for 15 minutes. Serves 6.

EVERYBODY'S IRISH

8 oz. Irish whiskey

4 oz. green Chartreuse
4 oz. green crème de menthe

Mix and pour over glasses of ice. Serves 4.

GREEN BEER

Pour beer into a pitcher. Stir in a few drops of green food coloring. Serve.

SALMON MOUSSE

1 T. unflavored gelatin
¼ C. cold water
1 C. sour cream, heated
1 lb. canned salmon
¼ C. mayonnaise

1 T. grated onion
1/3 C. celery, finely chopped
½ tsp. salt
¼ tsp. pepper
1 C. whipping cream, whipped

Soften the gelatin in the cold water. Add the sour cream. Cool. Add the rest of the ingredients, except the whipping cream. When the mixture begins to congeal, fold in the cream. Pour into a wet mold and chill. Serve with crackers.

IRISH STEW

2 T. butter
2 onions, chopped
3 lbs. boneless lamb stew meat, cut
  into 1-inch cubes
¾ tsp. dried thyme
½ t. salt
½ tsp. pepper
2 potatoes, peeled and sliced

3 C. chicken broth
½ tsp. Worcestershire sauce
4 potatoes, peeled and halved
8 carrots, peeled and sliced
¼ C. pearl barley
¼ C. heavy cream
Chopped fresh parsley

In a Dutch oven, add the butter and heat over medium heat. Add the onions until soft. Add the meat, thyme, salt, pepper, sliced potatoes, chicken broth, Worcestershire sauce and halved potatoes. Cover and bake in preheated 325 degrees F. oven for 1 hour. Remove from the oven and add the rest of the ingredients, except the parsley. Mix well and bake for 45 to 60 minutes more. Add the fresh parsley when ready to serve. Serves 4 to 6.

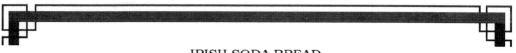

IRISH SODA BREAD

6 C. flour	1 T. + 1 tsp. sugar
1 T. baking powder	2 ½ C. buttermilk
2 tsp. baking soda	2 T. butter, melted
1 ½ tsp. salt	1 ½ C. raisins

Combine the first 5 ingredients in a large bowl. Mix well. Set aside. Combine the rest of the ingredients and add to the flour mixture. Stir until moistened. Turn dough out on a floured surface and knead for 5 minutes. Place on a greased baking sheet. Press dough evenly into a 1 ½ -inch-thick circle. Bake in a preheated 325 degrees F. oven for 1 hour. Remove to a wire rack. Cool 5 minutes and cut into wedges.

IRISH COFFEE

½ C. Irish whiskey	5 C. hot very strong coffee
½ C. Baileys liqueur	Whipping cream, whipped

Mix all ingredients, except whipping cream, and pour into coffee cups. Add the whipping cream on top. Serves 6.

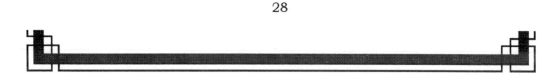

FLAMING PEARS

6 ripe pear
½ stick butter

Sugar
1 ½ oz. Irish Mist liqueur
1 ½ oz. gin

Peel and core the pears. Core them from the bottom so you can leave them whole. Melt the butter in a skillet. Add the pears upright in the skillet. Heat over medium heat for 5 minutes, basting with the butter. Place the pears in a buttered muffin pan and sprinkle the remaining butter over them. Sprinkle with sugar. Bake in preheated 500 degrees F. oven for 5 minutes. Place on serving plates. Combine the Irish Mist liqueur and gin in a skillet, and heat until hot. Ignite. While flaming, pour at once over the pears. Serves 6.

SHAMROCK COOKIES

½ C. sugar
2 sticks of butter
2 T. water

3 C. flour
1 can green decorator frosting

Beat together the sugar, butter and water. Add the flour gradually until well blended. Knead for 3 to 4 minutes. Roll out the dough to ¼ -inch thick on a well-floured board. Cut out with a shamrock cookie cutter. Bake on an ungreased cookie sheet. Bake in a preheated 350 degrees F. oven for 10 to 12 minutes. Ice with a green frosting. Makes 18.

NOTES

EASTER SUNDAY BRUNCH

POMEGRANATE AND ORANGE JUICE

MILK PUNCH

FRUIT WITH FRESH LIME JUICE DRESSING

BAKED HAM WITH ORANGE GLAZE

BAKED FRENCH TOAST

HASH BROWN POTATOES

WHITE CHOCOLATE BREAD PUDDING

COFFEE

"RELIGION IS A WAY OF WALKING, NOT
A WAY OF TALKING."
DEAN WILLIAM R. INGE

31

POMEGRANTE AND ORANGE DRINK

16 oz. fresh orange juice

8 oz. soda water
4 oz. pomegranate juice

Mix and serve in tall glasses over ice. Serves 4.

MILK PUNCH

6 C. milk
2 C. cream

6 T. sugar
16 jiggers bourbon
Nutmeg

Pour all the ingredients, except nutmeg, into a blender with a little ice and mix well. Pour into individual glasses or punch cups and sprinkle a little nutmeg on top. Serves 8.

FRUIT WITH FRESH LIME JUICE DRESSING

¼ C. fresh lime juice
¾ C. oil

2 tsp. grated lime peel
1 tsp. salt
2 T. parsley, chopped

Mix all the ingredients. Pour over fruit of your choice and refrigerate for at least 30 minutes or longer.

BAKED HAM WITH ORANGE GLAZE

1-5 to 6 lb. ham
¼ C. sugar
2 T. cornstarch
1½ C. orange juice

1/3 C. horseradish
2 T. cider vinegar
1½ tsp. orange peel, grated
¼ tsp. salt

Insert a meat thermometer into center of the ham. Place on a rack in a shallow roasting pan. Preheat oven to 325 degrees F. and bake for 2 hours or until meat thermometer reaches 140 degrees F. In a small saucepan, stir sugar and cornstarch. Add remaining ingredients and cook over medium heat until the mixture thickens and starts to boil. Remove from heat. After the ham has cooked 1½ hours, brush ham with orange glaze every 10 minutes. Serves 18 to 22.

BAKED FRENCH TOAST

1 loaf French bread, sliced into 8-
  2 inch slices

1 C. maple syrup

Pour syrup into a large greased baking pan. Place the bread on top of the syrup.

3 whole eggs
3 egg whites

1 ½ C. milk
2 tsp. vanilla extract
¼ tsp. nutmeg

In a bowl, mix all the ingredients well. Pour over bread and push down to soak all the bread. Cover and refrigerate overnight. Sprinkle nutmeg over mixture. Cook in a preheat 350 degrees F. oven for 40 to 45 minutes. Serves 8.

HASH BROWN POTATOES

Bake potato, 1 per person,
  shredded
¼ C. butter

Salt and pepper to taste
½ tsp. paprika

In a skillet over medium heat, melt butter. Add potato and fry 15 minutes or until browned, turning occasionally. Remove and add the rest of ingredients.

WHITE CHOCOLATE BREAD PUDDING

½ loaf French bread, cut into ¼ inch
   slices and crust cut off
1 ½ C. half and half
½ C. whipping cream

1 large whole egg
4 large egg yolks
½ C. sugar
1 ½ tsp. vanilla extract
4 oz. white chocolate, melted in a
   double boiler

Butter an 8x8-inch baking dish. Bake the bread on a cookie sheet at 350 degrees F. for 10 minutes. Line the baking dish on the sides and bottom with the baked bread. Heat the half and half and cream in a medium saucepan over low heat until hot. Do not boil. Beat egg, egg yolks and sugar in a small bowl. Whisk a few tablespoons warm cream mixture into egg mixture. Whisk eggs back into cream. Stir in vanilla. Place melted chocolate into a large bowl and slowly whisk cream mixture into it. Strain custard into baking dish and let the bread absorb the mixture. Place baking dish in a larger pan with a large rim. Fill the larger pan with at least 1 inch of boiling water. Bake in a preheated 350 degrees F. oven for 35 to 45 minutes. Insert a knife and it will be done if it comes out clean. Check after 15 minutes and add more boiling water if needed. Add the white chocolate sauce.

White chocolate sauce:

¾ C. heavy cream

4 oz. white chocolate, melted in a
   double boiler
Shavings of dark and milk chocolate

Heat cream until frothy, but not boiling. Whisk warm cream into melted chocolate until smooth. Refrigerate until ready to use. Reheat. Pour over bread pudding when ready to serve. Serves 6.

NOTES

EASTER CELEBRATION

LEMON FRAPPE   RED WINE SPRITZER

GREEK EASTER EGGS

HAM WITH PINEAPPLE SAUCE

ASPARAGUS VINAIGRETTE

PARSLEY RICE   BRUSSELS SPROUTS

WHOLE WHEAT DINNER ROLLS

COCONUT CREAM CAKE

COFFEE

HE HAS RISEN.

LEMON FRAPPE

1-6 oz. can frozen lemonade
2 C. water

1 pint lemon sherbet
1-12 oz. bottle ginger ale

Combine the first 3 ingredients in a blender and blend until smooth. Pour into a pitcher and add the ginger ale. Serve in champagne glasses. Makes 1 ½ quarts.

RED WINE SPRITZER

3 C. chilled red wine

1 C. chilled club soda

Combine the two and serve over ice. Serves 4.

GREEK EASTER EGGS

Spicy Salt:

2 T. salt
½ tsp. garlic salt

1 tsp. ground black pepper
¾ tsp. paprika
2 T. finely chopped parsley

Combine all the ingredients and place in several small bowls.

2 dozen eggs

red vegetable dye

Boil eggs for 15 minutes and cool them. Dye them with the red vegetable dye. Refrigerate until ready to serve.

Tradition:

The head of the household cracks an egg against the egg of one of the guest, saying as he does it, "Christ is risen." The response is, "He is risen, indeed." Each person tries to crack another egg, keeping his own intact. The victory goes to the one whose egg remains intact after everybody else's is cracked. After this has taken place, each person peels his egg and dips it in the salt.

HAM WITH PINEAPPLE SAUCE

1-4 to 6 lb. boneless ham

Insert a meat thermometer into the ham and place on a rack in a shallow baking pan. Bake in a preheated 325 degrees F. oven for 1½ hours to 2 ½ hours until the thermometer registers 140 degrees F.

Sauce:

½ C. finely chopped onion
¼ C. butter

1 C. catsup
1 C. pineapple preserves
2 tsp. dry mustard

Cook the onion in the butter until tender. Add the rest of the ingredients and heat. Brush the sauce on the ham before serving. Serves 16 to 18.

ASPARAGUS VINAIGRETTE

2 ½ lbs. fresh asparagus

Cook asparagus for 10 minutes or until tender. Drain and refrigerate. An hour before serving, pour vinaigrette sauce over the asparagus and refrigerate until ready to serve. Serves 8 to 10.

Sauce:

6 T. olive oil
1 tsp. dry mustard
1 tsp. parsley flakes
1 tsp. chopped fresh chives
1 tsp. capers, chopped

1 hard-boiled egg, chopped
3 T. wine vinegar
Salt and pepper to taste
½ tsp. tarragon leaves
1 tsp. garlic salt
1 C. water

Mix all the ingredients together.

PARSLEY RICE

4 T. butter
1 onion, diced
2 C. long-grain rice

4 C. canned chicken stock
1 tsp. salt
¼ C. fresh parsley, minced

In a medium saucepan melt the butter. Add the onions and cook until tender. Add the rice and cook for 1 minute. Pour the chicken stock and salt into the onions. With heat on high, bring the mixture to a boil, uncovered. Cover and simmer for 20 minutes. Add the parsley and stir. Cover and simmer 2 minutes. Place in a serving bowl. Serves 8.

BRUSSELS SPROUTS

2 lb. Brussels sprouts
8 oz. bacon, fried and diced

2 T. flour
2 C. chicken broth
1 C. chopped onions

Blanch the sprouts for 10 to 12 minutes in salted boiling water. Drain all but 2 teaspoons of the grease, from frying the bacon. Sprinkle with flour and cook 2 minutes. Add the broth, onions and sprouts. Reduce heat and simmer gently until thickened. Pour over the spouts. Makes 8 servings.

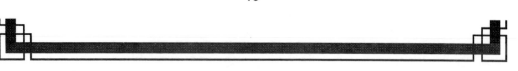

WHOLE WHEAT DINNER ROLLS

2 C. warm water
¾ C. oil
1 ½ T. molasses
2 pkg. yeast
4 to 4 ½ C. flour

3 C. whole-wheat flour
¼ C. sugar
2 tsp. salt
2 eggs
Melted butter

In hot water, add the oil, molasses and yeast. Mix. Add 2 cups of the white flour, 1 cup whole-wheat flour and remaining ingredients, except melted butter. With a mixer on medium speed, beat for 5 minutes. With a wooden spoon, add in the rest of the whole wheat flour. Mix. Mix in the rest of the white flour until stiff dough forms. On a well-floured surface, knead the dough for 5 minutes. Place in a greased bowl, cover and let rise until doubled. This takes about 1 hour. Grease one large baking sheet. Punch down the dough and shape into 36 balls. Arrange on the baking sheet. Cover and let rise until doubled. This takes about 45 minutes. Bake in a preheated 375 degrees F. oven for 15 to 20 minutes. Brush with melted butter when done. Makes 36 rolls.

COCONUT CREAM CAKE

½ C. shortening
1 stick margarine
2 C. sugar
5 egg yolks, save the whites

1 tsp. baking soda
2 c. flour
1 C. buttermilk
1 2/3 C. coconut

Grease three 8-inch round cake pans. Preheat oven to 350 degrees F. Beat the egg whites until stiff and set aside. Beat shortening, margarine and sugar until fluffy. Add egg yolks one at a time beating after each egg. Add baking soda and blend. Add flour alternately with buttermilk. Add coconut and blend. Fold in beaten egg whites. Pour into prepared pans and bake about 30 minutes. Cool and remove from pans and frost.

Frosting:

1 stick margarine, softened
1-8 oz. pkg. cream cheese, softened
1 box powdered sugar

¼ tsp. salt
2 tsp. vanilla
1 C. pecans, chopped

Cream margarine and cream cheese. Add sugar, salt, vanilla and beat. Fold in pecans and spread on cool cake.

42

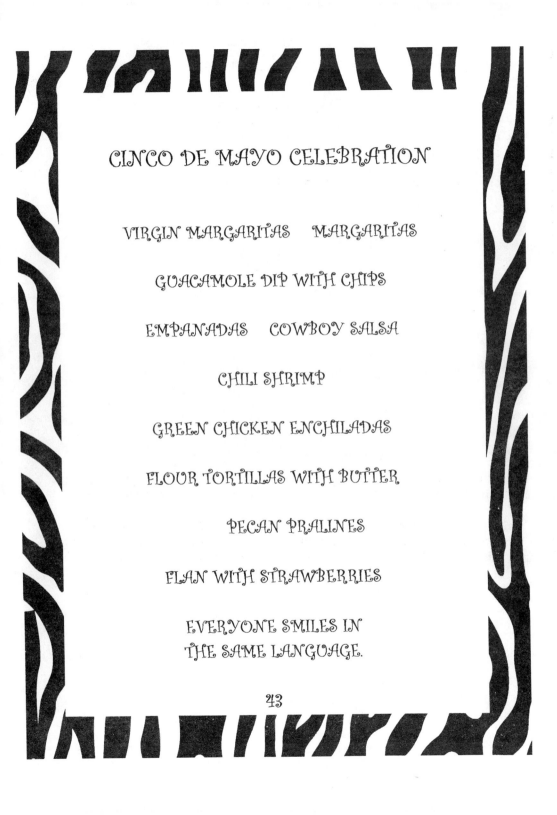

CINCO DE MAYO CELEBRATION

VIRGIN MARGARITAS   MARGARITAS

GUACAMOLE DIP WITH CHIPS

EMPANADAS   COWBOY SALSA

CHILI SHRIMP

GREEN CHICKEN ENCHILADAS

FLOUR TORTILLAS WITH BUTTER

PECAN PRALINES

FLAN WITH STRAWBERRIES

EVERYONE SMILES IN
THE SAME LANGUAGE.

VIRGIN MARGARITAS

2 oz. lime juice   6 oz. sour mix
2 oz. orange juice

Mix together and pour over ice. Serves 4.

MARGARITAS

Salt   1 ½ oz. fresh lime juice
4 oz. crushed ice   1 oz. Cointreau or Triple Sec
2 oz. white tequila   1 lime cut in wedges

Circle the rim of the glass with the lime wedge, and then dip the rim in salt.
Combine all remaining ingredients in a blender and blend until frothy. Pour
into the glass and serve immediately. Serve with a lime slice. Serves 1.

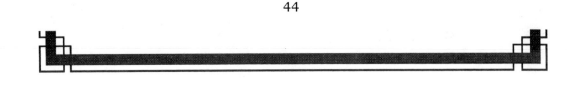

EMPANADAS

You can make the empanadas earlier and cook right before serving.

1 pkg. 10 oz. frozen patty shells

Filling:

½ lb. lean ground pork
¼ C. minced onion
3 T. raisins
3 T. chopped ripe olives
3 T. chili sauce

½ ground coriander
1 tsp. chili powder
½ tsp. ground cumin
½ tsp. garlic salt
Salt and pepper to taste

Brown the meat and onion in a frying pan over medium heat. Add the remaining ingredients.

Thaw the patty shells about 30 minutes. Slightly overlap them on a slightly floured board and roll out to 1/8-inch thickness. With a cookie cutter cut dough into 3 ½ -inch rounds. Place a slightly rounded teaspoon of the filling on each round, fold in half, moisten edges with water and press together with a fork to seal. Place turnover 1-inch apart on ungreased baking sheets. Prick tops with a fork and bake in a preheated oven at 400 degrees F. for 7 to 8 minutes. Makes about 2 dz. turnovers.

GUACAMOLE DIP

6 ripe avocados
½ C. picante sauce
½ C. sour cream

½ t. garlic salt
1 T. lemon juice
1 tomato, chopped

This should be made earlier in the day to chill.
Mash avocados with a fork. Stir in picante sauce, sour cream, garlic salt and lemon juice. Place mixture in a blender and puree. Stir in chopped tomatoes by hand. Refrigerate. If you will place the pit of the avocado in the mixture until serving, it will keep the guacamole from turning brown. Serves 8 to 10.

COWBOY SALSA

2 large tomatoes, chopped
1 large onion, chopped
2 large jalapenos, chopped and seeded

1 T. vinegar
1 T. oil
Garlic salt

Add all the ingredients together and mix. Refrigerate.

CHILI SHRIMP

1 ½ lb. uncooked medium shrimp,
  peeled and deveined
¾ C. olive oil
1/3 C. white wine vinegar
3 T. fresh lemon juice

2 T. Dijon mustard
1 ½ T. tomato puree
2 tsp. chili powder
Salt and peeper
¼ C. finely chopped cilantro

Drop the shrimp into a large pot of boiling water and cook just until light pink, about 4 minutes. Rinse in cool water and pat dry. Place the shrimp in a shallow glass dish. Whisk the remaining ingredients, except the cilantro. Pour over the shrimp and toss well. Cover with plastic wrap and refrigerate overnight. Sprinkle the cilantro on top. Serve chilled. Make this one day in advance. Serves 6.

GREEN CHICKEN ENCHILADAS

1 chicken, cooked, skin removed and
  and chopped
¼ C. chicken stock
3 medium green tomatoes
1 can whole green chilies
2 large garlic cloves, minced
1 jalapeno pepper, seeded and coarsely
  chopped

1/3 C. cilantro leaves
Salt and pepper to taste
1 C. heavy cream
1 egg
12 corn tortillas
½ C. sour cream, whisked

Place the chicken and chicken stock in a saucepan and keep warm over low heat. Boil the tomatoes for 15 minutes. Peel. Combine the tomatoes, chilies, garlic, jalapeno and cilantro in the container of a processor and puree. Add salt and pepper. Pour in a pan. Beat the cream with the egg until well blended. Add to the puree. Heat on low heat. Heat a little oil in a skillet and briefly fry one tortilla to soften. Dip one side of the tortilla in the puree. Spoon some chicken on the coated side. Roll up tightly and place in a baking dish just large enough to fit 12 enchiladas. Repeat until all 12 tortillas are done. Pour the remaining puree over the enchiladas. Bake in a preheated 350 degrees F. oven for 15 minutes. Drizzle the sour cream over the enchiladas and serve hot. Serves 6.

FLOUR TORTILLAS

Wrap as many flour tortillas in heavy-duty foil, as you need. Place in oven at 350 degrees F. until hot. Serve with butter.

FLAN WITH FRESH STRAWBERRIES

1 pt. strawberries, sliced   2 T. sugar

Place strawberries in a bowl and sprinkle with the sugar. Cover with plastic and refrigerate until ready to serve.

1 C. sugar   2 C. water
6 eggs, well-beaten   1 tsp. almond extract
1 can sweetened condensed milk   Whipping cream, whipped

Place sugar in a large, heavy iron skillet, caramelize by cooking over medium heat, stirring constantly with a wooden spoon until sugar melts and turns golden brown. Pour and spread quickly on bottom and sides of ungreased 10x6-inch baking dish. Cool. In a large bowl, mix eggs, milk, water and almond extract. Pour into dish. Bake in a preheated 350 degrees F. oven for 1 hour. Cool at least 2 hours and serve with the strawberries and whipping cream on top of each serving. Serves 6 to 8 servings.

PECAN PRALINES

1 ½ C. brown sugar   2 T. butter
1 ½ C. white sugar   2 C. pecan halves
1 C. evaporated milk   1 tsp. vanilla

Cook sugars and evaporated milk until a soft ball forms in cold water. Remove from heat and add butter. Beat until creamy. Add pecans and vanilla. Drop on waxed paper. Makes 30 pralines.

MOTHER'S DAY BRUNCH

ORANGE JULIUS   MIMOSA

BROWN SUGAR BAKED BACON

SPINACH AND CHEESE QUICHE

HOME FRIES

AVOCADO AND GRAPEFRUIT SALAD
WITH POPPY SEED DRESSING

APPLE WALNUT MUFFINS

BUTTERMILK CINNAMON ROLLS

COFFEE

"MOTHER IS THE NAME FOR GOD IN THE LIPS
AND HEARTS OF CHILDREN."
WILLIAM MAKEPEACH THACKERAY

49

ORANGE JULIUS

1-6 oz. can frozen orange juice concentrate	½ tsp. vanilla extract
	1 C. water
¼ C. sugar	12 ice cubes

Mix all ingredients in a blender. Serve immediately. Serves 4 to 6.

MIMOSAS

1 part champagne, chilled   1 part orange juice, chilled

Combine and fill chilled champagne glasses.

BROWN SUGAR BAKED BACON

12 slices thick-sliced bacon   ½ C. brown sugar

Dip bacon slices in brown sugar. Place on a boiler pan. Bake in a preheated 375 degrees F. oven for 20 to 25 minutes or until bacon is crisp.

SPINACH AND CHEESE QUICHE

Quiche Crust:

2 C. flour
1 tsp. salt
2 tsp. baking powder

½ C. oil
¼ C. milk

Mix the flour, salt and baking powder together. Mix the oil and milk together, and then pour into the flour. Stir only until mixed. The mixture will be rather coarse and granular. Do not over mix. Mold into two balls and wrap with plastic. Allow to sit for 15 minutes. Each ball will make one 9-inch piecrust. Roll out between two sheets of wax paper. Place the pastry in the pie plate and prick the bottom with a kitchen fork.

Filling:

1-8 oz. cream cheese
1 T. butter
½ C. chopped onions
1 C. sliced fresh mushrooms

1 bunch spinach, wash and drain
¼ lb. grated Swiss cheese
5 large eggs
1 C. half and half

Cover the bottom of the crust with the cream cheese, cut into small pieces. Saute the onions in the butter until transparent. Add the spinach and mushrooms to the onions. Spread on top of the cream cheese and top with the cheese. Mix the eggs and half and half together and pour over the top. Bake in a preheated 425 degrees F. oven for 15 minutes, reduce heat to 350 degrees F. and bake for 30 minutes.

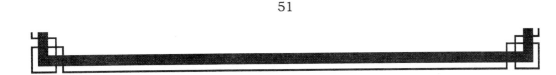

HOME FRIES

3 T. butter
3 medium potatoes, thinly sliced
1/8 tsp. garlic powder

¼ tsp. salt
1/8 tsp. pepper
1 small onion, thinly sliced and
   separated into rings

In a large skillet melt butter. Layer potatoes in the skillet. Sprinkle with garlic powder, salt and pepper. Cook, covered, over medium heat for 8 minutes. Add onion rings. Cook, uncovered, 8 to 10 minutes till potatoes are tender and browned, turning frequently. Makes 4 servings.

AVOCADO-GRAPEFRUIT SALAD WITH POPPY SEED DRESSING

2 large pink grapefruit, peeled and section
12 fresh strawberries, cut in half
1 apple, peeled, cored and sliced

2 large ripe avocados, peeled and
   sliced
Poppy-seed dressing
Lettuce

Place the fruit on the lettuce. Pour the poppy-seed dressing over top. Serve immediately. Serves 6.

POPPY-SEED DRESSING

1 ½ C. sugar
2 tsp. dry mustard
1 ½ tsp. salt
2/3 C. white or wine vinegar

3 T. onion juice
2 C. salad oil
3 T. poppy seeds

Mix sugar, mustard, salt and vinegar in a bowl. Add onion juice and stir. Slowly add oil, beating constantly until thickened. Stir in poppy seeds and store in refrigerator until ready to use. Stir well and allow to reach room temperature before serving. Makes 3 ½ cups.

APPLE WALNUT MUFFINS

1 ½ C. all-purpose flour
2 tsp. baking powder
1 ½ tsp. ground cinnamon
1 tsp. baking soda
½ tsp. salt

2 large eggs
¾ C. sugar
1 ½ C. finely paced chopped
 peeled apples
5 T. warm melted butter
½ C. chopped walnuts

Whisk together the first 5 ingredients. In a separate bowl add the eggs and sugar and whisk thoroughly. Let stand 10 minutes. Stir in the dry ingredients until the dry ingredients are moistened. Do not over mix. Stir in the apples, butter and walnuts. Mix. The batter will not be smooth. Grease a 12 muffin pan and pour mixture to about halfway. Preheat oven to 400 degrees F. Cook for 14 to 16 minutes. Remove from oven and cool on a rack.

BUTTERMILK CINNAMON ROLLS

2 pkgs. dry yeast
¼ C. warm water
1 ½ C. buttermilk
½ C. vegetable oil
4 ½ C. flour

1 tsp. salt
½ tsp. baking soda
½ C. butter, melted
1 ¼ C. brown sugar
2 tsp. ground cinnamon

In a large bowl, dissolve yeast in warm water. Let stand until creamy, about 10 minutes. In a small saucepan, heat the buttermilk until warm but do not boil. Pour the buttermilk and oil into the yeast mixture and mix well. Combine the flour, salt and baking soda. Stir the flour mixture into the liquid 1 cup at a time, until soft dough forms. Turn dough out onto a lightly floured surface and knead 20 times. Cover and let rest for 15 minutes. In a small bowl, stir together the butter, brown sugar and cinnamon. On a lightly floured surface, roll dough out into a large rectangle. Spread the brown sugar and butter mixture over the dough, roll up into a log and pinch the seam to seal. Slice into 1-inch pieces and place cut side up in a lightly greased 10x15-inch baking pan. Cover and let rise 30 minutes or cover and refrigerate overnight. If baking immediately, preheat oven to 400 degrees F. Bake for 20 to 25 minutes, until golden brown. Makes 15.

NOTES

KENTUCKY DERBY BREAKFAST

LADY LARK   MINT JULEP

BAKED HAM OMELET

CURRIED HOT FRUIT

CHEESE GRITS   FRIED GREEN TOMATOES

PINA COLADA MUFFINS   MANGO BREAD

BUTTERMILK BISCUITS

COFFEE

"ALL HAPPINESS DEPENDS ON A
LEISURELY BREAKFAST."
JOHN GAUNTER

55

LADY LARK

4 C. orange juice, chilled   ¼ C. cranberry juice, chilled
                                     Fresh strawberries

Mix orange juice and cranberry juice together. Pour in a glass and add a
strawberry. Serves 4.

MINT JULEP

1 tsp. sugar   3 oz. bourbon
Fresh mint sprigs   Crushed ice

Place a few drops water in a glass and add 4 mint sprigs and sugar. Dissolve
the sugar. Take the sprigs out of the glass. Almost fill the glass with crushed
ice. Add the bourbon. Garnish with a mint sprig. Servers 1.

BAKED HAM OMELET

½ loaf white bread, cubed   2 C. milk
1 ¼ lb. cheddar cheese, grated   Salt and pepper to taste
1 C. cooked ham, cubed   1 can chopped green chilies
8 eggs   ¼ C. green onion, chopped

Place bread cubes in a greased 9x13-inch baking pan. Sprinkle with half of the
ham and half of the cheese. Repeat. In a large bowl, beat eggs, milk, salt,
pepper, green chilies and onions. Pour over egg mixture. Place on a larger pan
with a rim. Pour water into a larger pan and cook in a preheated 350 degrees F.
oven for 60 minutes or until eggs have set. Serves 12.

CURRIED HOT FRUIT

Carol Adams, Fort Stockton, TX

5 ½ T. butter, melted
¾ C. brown sugar
2 tsp. curry powder

1 tall can pears
1 tall can cling peach halves
1 tall can apricots, plus #2 can
(medium)

Drain fruit. Make syrup of first three ingredients. Place fruit in a baking dish and pour syrup over the fruits. Bake in a preheated oven at 350 degrees F. for 1 hour the day before. Reheat before serving.

CHEESE GRITS

Carol Adams, Fort Stockton, TX

1 C. uncooked grits, cook according to
instructions
1 roll garlic cheese

1 egg, beaten in a cup then fill
with milk
1 stick butter, melted

Mix all together. Put in a casserole dish and bake in a preheated oven at 350 degrees F. for 45 minutes.

57

FRIED GREEN TOMATOES

2 green tomatoes, cut in 1-inch slices
1 C. flour

Salt and pepper to taste
½ C. butter

Mix the flour, salt and pepper. Dip the tomato slices in the flour mixture. Melt the butter in a skillet and sauté the tomato slices until brown. Serves 6.

PINA COLADA MUFFINS

1 egg, beaten
2 C. buttermilk baking mix
½ C. crushed pineapple, drained

¾ C. shredded coconut
2 T. sugar
2/3 C. orange juice
2 T. oil

Mix all ingredients together. Pour into muffin cups that have been greased on the bottom only. Bake in a preheated 400 degrees F. oven for 15 minutes or until golden brown. Spread with the rum glaze. Makes 12 muffins.

Glaze:

¾ C. powdered sugar

½ tsp. rum extract
2 to 3 tsp. milk.

Mix together and spread over muffins.

MANGO BREAD

2 C. flour
2 tsp. baking soda
¼ tsp. salt
1 ½ C. sugar
2 tsp. cinnamon

3 eggs, beaten
¾ C. vegetable oil
2 C. mango, finely chopped
¾ C. pecans, chopped
1 T. lime juice

In a bowl, combine the dry ingredients and mix. Make a well in the center of the mixture and add the eggs and oil. Stir until moistened. Sir in the rest of the ingredients. Pour into 2 greased loaf pans. Preheat oven to 375 degrees F. and bake for 1 hour. Cool on wire racks. Makes 2 loaves.

BUTTERMILK BISCUITS

2 C. flour
1 T. baking powder
½ tsp. salt
½ tsp. baking soda

½ C. shortening
1 egg, beaten
1 C. buttermilk

In a bowl, combine dry ingredients. Cut in the shortening. Blend in the egg and buttermilk. Mix until you can make a ball. Roll dough out on a floured board. The dough should be ½ -inch thick. Cut out with a 2-inch biscuit cutter. Place in a greased pan. Bake in a preheated 450 degrees F. oven for 12 to 15 minutes. Makes 16.

NOTES

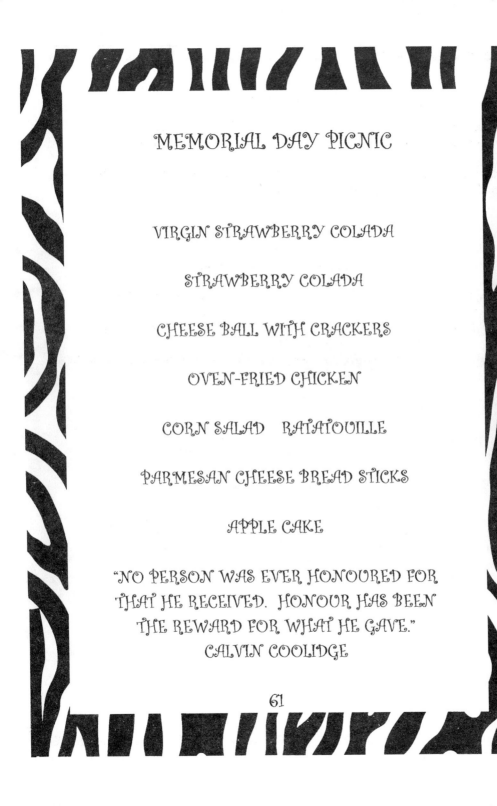

MEMORIAL DAY PICNIC

VIRGIN STRAWBERRY COLADA

STRAWBERRY COLADA

CHEESE BALL WITH CRACKERS

OVEN-FRIED CHICKEN

CORN SALAD   RATATOUILLE

PARMESAN CHEESE BREAD STICKS

APPLE CAKE

"NO PERSON WAS EVER HONOURED FOR
THAT HE RECEIVED. HONOUR HAS BEEN
THE REWARD FOR WHAT HE GAVE."
CALVIN COOLIDGE

61

VIRGIN STRAWBERRY COLADA

28 strawberries
20 oz. pineapple juice

4 C. crushed ice
6 oz. coconut cream

Blend all the ingredients in a blender. Pour into a glass and garnish with a maraschino cherry and pineapple wedge. Serves 4.

STRAWBERRY COLADA

4 oz. dark rum
4 oz. light rum
20 ripe strawberries

16 oz. pineapple juice
4 oz. coconut cream
4 C. crushed ice

Blend all the ingredients in a blender. Pour into a glass and garnish with a maraschino cherry and pineapple wedge. Serves 4.

CHEESE BALL

Sherry Workman, Mesa, AZ.

1-8 oz. cream cheese, softened
1 stick of butter, softened
1 small can of olives, chopped

1 bunch of green onions, chopped
1 T. Worcestershire sauce
Chopped pecans

Mix all together, except pecans. Refrigerate a least one hour. Roll in the pecans before serving. Lasts up to a week in the refrigerator.

OVEN-FRIED CHICKEN WITH PARMESAN CHEESE

This coats about 12 pieces of chicken. Depending on how may people you will serve, will determine how many pieces of chicken you will need.

Mix in a bowl:
1 C. milk
1 C. sour cream

½ C. Dijon mustard
1 T. minced garlic

Mix in a bowl:
3 C. dry unseasoned breadcrumbs
1 C. grated Parmesan cheese

1 tsp. sage
1 tsp. dried oregano
Salt and pepper to taste

Coat each piece of chicken in the milk mixture and then roll in the crumb mixture. Place the chicken on a greased baking sheet. Bake in a preheated 350 degrees F. oven for 45 to 60 minutes. This can be served hot or at room temperature for the picnic.

CORN SALAD

5 ears fresh corn
1 small red onion, minced
1-4 oz. jar pimentos, chopped and
   drained
1 T. brown sugar

½ tsp. celery seeds
½ tsp dry mustard
Salt and pepper to taste
3 T. vinegar
2 T. olive oil

Cut the kernels off the cob. The easy way to cut the kernels off is to put one end of the corn in the hole of a bunt pan and cut off the kernels. Put the kernels in a bowl and place ½ cup water in the bowl and cover. Microwave on high for 45 seconds. Drain. Add the minced onion and pimentos. Add the rest of ingredients, cover and refrigerate. This will keep up to one week. Serves 6.

RATATOUILLE

3 zucchini, sliced
1 eggplant, peeled and sliced
4 tomatoes, peeled and diced
2 green peppers, sliced thin

1 C. onion, thinly sliced
¼ C. salad oil
1 clove garlic, minced
1 tsp. salt and pepper

Saute the onion in the oil until soft. Add tomatoes, cook 1 minute. Mix in the rest of the ingredients, cover and bring to a boil. Cook 5 minutes. Remove cover and simmer until all liquid has evaporated. Refrigerate until time to take to the picnic. Keeps for several days. Serves 4.

PARMESAN CHEESE BREAD STICKS

1 1/3 C. warm water
2 T. sugar
2 pkg. dry yeast

2 tsp. salt
4 T. oil
4 C. flour
½ C. Parmesan cheese, grated

Mix water, sugar and yeast. Add salt, oil, 3 cups flour and cheese. Beat with mixer 4 to 5 minutes. Add more flour as needed. Place ½ cup of flour on board and knead into dough. Make a medium stiff dough. Knead until very smooth and satiny. Place in an oiled bowl. Cover and let rise until doubled. Punch down and let rest 10 minutes. Cut dough in half and cut each half into 32 pieces. Roll one at a time into pencil-size rope. Place ¾ inches apart on an oiled pan. Let rise until doubled. Bake in preheated 325 degrees F. oven for 25 minutes or until brown. Spray the bread sticks with water cooking for 5 more minutes. Repeat and cook for 10 minutes. Cool and store in airtight containers. Makes 64.

APPLE CAKE

½ C. shortening
1 C. sugar
½ C. firmly packed brown sugar
2 tsp. soda
1 C. buttermilk
2 eggs, beaten

2 ¼ C. flour
½ tsp. salt
½ tsp. nutmeg
½ tsp. cinnamon
¼ tsp. cloves
2 C. apples, peeled and chopped

Cream shortening, sugar and brown sugar. Dissolve soda in buttermilk. Stir into shortening mixture. Add eggs, flour, spices and salt. Beat until thoroughly mixed. Fold in apples. Pour into a greased 13x9-inch pan. Mix the topping together and sprinkle on top of the batter. Bake in a preheated 350 degrees F. oven for 35 to 45 minutes. Be sure that a knife inserted comes out clean. Serves 12 to 15.

Topping:

½ C. pecans, chopped
¼ C. sugar

¼ C. brown sugar, firmly packed
¼ tsp. cinnamon

Mix together all the ingredients. Sprinkle on top of batter.

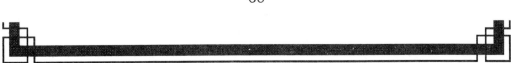

NOTES

FATHER'S DAY COOK OUT

SHIRLEY TEMPLE   ROY ROGERS

BOURBON SLUSH   BEER

SAUSAGE DIP WITH CHIPS

BARBEQUED CHEESEBURGERS

CAESAR POTATO SALAD

GRILLED CORN ON THE COB

BROWN SUGAR BOURBON PEACHES
WITH VANILLA ICE CREAM

SUGAR COOKIES

"THE MOST IMPORTANT THING A FATHER CAN
DO FOR HIS CHILDREN IS TO LOVE THEIR MOTHER."
THEODORE HESBURGH

SHIRLEY TEMPLE

6 oz. lemon-line soda

1 dash grenadine syrup
1 maraschino cherry

Pour all ingredients in a glass with ice. Serves 1.

ROY ROGER

6 oz. cola

1 dash grenadine syrup
1 maraschino cherry

Pour all ingredients in a glass with ice. Serves 1.

BOURBON SLUSH

9 C. water
3 C. bourbon
1-12 oz. can frozen orange juice, thawed
1-12 oz. can frozen lemonade, thawed

1 ¾ C. sugar
1 T. instant tea
3-16 oz. bottles lemon-lime soda

Mix all ingredients except the soda. Freeze. When ready to serve, spoon the slush in a glass and pour the soda over the mixture.

SAUSAGE DIP

1 lb. ground beef
1 lb. pork sausage
1 onion, chopped
2 lbs. Velveeta cheese, cubed

1 can Rotel's green chilies and
   tomatoes
1 can mushroom soup
1 tsp. garlic powder

Brown beef and sausage with the chopped onion. Add Velveeta cheese. After cheese has melted, add remaining ingredients. Serve hot with chips.

BARBEQUED CHEESEBURGERS

1 T. Worcestershire sauce
1 T. Lowry's seasoned salt

3 lbs. lean ground round steak
12 slices cheddar cheese

Mix all ingredients, except the cheese, together in a large bowl. Form into 12 patties. Place on grill. Grill on one side and turn. Add a slice of cheese to each one. Grill until done.

CAESAR-STYLE POTATO SALAD

½ C. salad oil
¼ C. grated Parmesan cheese
¼ C. lemon juice
Salt and pepper to taste
1 T. Worcestershire sauce

5 lbs. potatoes, cooked & diced
8 bacon slices, fried and crumbled
1 medium onion, chopped
¼ C. chopped parsley
2 hard-cooked eggs, sliced

About 3 hours before serving, combine first 6 ingredients in a large bowl and whisk. Add potatoes, bacon, onion and parsley to mixture. Toss gently to mix well. Arrange egg slices on top. Cover and refrigerate. Makes 8 to 10 servings.

GRILLED CORN ON THE COB

Remove the corn from husks and silk. Spread each ear with softened butter. Cut a double thickness of heavy-duty aluminum foil large enough to place an ear on each piece. Fold over and seal firmly. Place on grill and cook 20 minutes, turning the packets several times. Unfold packages and sprinkle with salt.

BROWN SUGAR-BOURBON PEACHES WITH VANILLA ICE CREAM

Pat Snyder, Dallas, TX.

12 T. bourbon
½ C. firmly packed dark brown sugar
4 T. butter
2 T. fresh lemon juice

2 tsp. vanilla
4 peaches, peeled, pitted and sliced
Vanilla ice cream

Place the first 5 ingredients in a heavy skillet over medium-low heat. Stir until sugar dissolves. Add peaches and stir until heated through. Serve over ice cream. Serves 4.

SUGAR COOKIES

Lynn Franklin, El Paso, TX..

2/3 C. shortening
¾ C. sugar
½ tsp. grated orange peel
½ tsp. vanilla
1 egg

4 tsp. milk
2 C. sifted flour
1 ½ tsp. baking powder
¼ tsp. salt

Thoroughly cream shortening, sugar, orange peel and vanilla. Add egg and beat till light and fluffy. Stir in milk. Sift together dry ingredients and blend into creamed mixture. Divide dough in half and chill 1 hour. On lightly floured surface, roll to 1/8 inch thickness. Cut in desired shapes with a cutter. Bake on a greased cookie sheet in a preheated 375 degrees F. oven for 6 to 8 minutes or golden brown. Remove from pan and cool on rack. Make 2 dozen cookies.

WEDDING BUFFET

WEDDING PUNCH   CHAMPAGNE PUNCH

CRAB AND WATER CHESTNUT APPETIZER
SPINACH TRIANGLES

ROAST BEEF WITH BLUE CHEESE MARINADE
BAKED HAM WITH CHAMPAGNE SAUCE

BIBB LETTUCE WITH BLUE CHEESE DRESSING
ARTICHOKE MUSHROOM SALAD
CHAMPAGNE FRUIT SALAD

BABY LIMA BEANS   SWEET POTATO BALLS
WILD RICE CASSEROLE

CHOCOLATE COVERED STRAWBERRIES
ITALIAN CREAM WEDDING CAKE

"LOVE LOOKS NOT WITH THE EYES, BUT
WITH THE HEART."
SHAKESPEARE

71

WEDDING RECEPTION PUNCH

4 C. tea
4 C. sugar
12 oz. orange juice

1-46 oz. can pineapple juice
12 C. water
1-12 oz. lemonade
3 bottles ginger ale

Dissolve the sugar in the tea. Add rest of the ingredients and pour into a punch bowl with an ice ring or crushed ice. Try the ice mold in the recipe below for the champagne wedding punch. Makes 40 punch cup servings.

CHAMPAGNE WEDDING PUNCH

Ice mold:

1 bunch green grapes

1 box strawberries

Fill an ice mold half full with water and freeze. When frozen, place the grapes and strawberries on top and cover with water. Place back in freezer. When ready to use dip mold briefly in warm water and unmold. Place on a piece of foil. You can replace in freezer or use immediately.

Punch:

25.4 oz. bottle sauterne
1 C. brandy
¼ C. sugar

32 oz. bottle club soda, chilled
2-4/5 qt. bottles dry champagne,
    chilled

Mix sauterne, brandy and sugar. Make sure sugar is dissolved. This can be kept in the refrigerator overnight. When ready to serve, pour in a punch bowl and add the ice mold. Pour in soda and champagne. Makes 28 punch bowl cups servings.

CRAB AND WATER CHESTNUT APPETIZER

2 C. fresh, frozen, or canned crabmeat
½ C. water chestnuts, chopped finely
2 T. soy sauce

½ C. mayonnaise
2 T. green onions, chopped finely
½ tsp. salt

Mix all the ingredients together. Place on melba toast rounds or crackers.
Serves 36.

SPINACH TRIANGLES

Filling:

2-10 oz. pkg. frozen chopped spinach
1 C. onion, chopped
¼ tsp. salt

2 cloves garlic, minced
12 oz. feta cheese, finely crumbled
1 tsp. crushed dried oregano

Cook spinach, onion, salt and garlic according to the spinach directions. Drain
well. Be sure to get all the moisture out. Mix the spinach, cheese and oregano.

Dough:
24 sheets phyllo dough

1 C. butter, melted

Brush a sheet of phyllo with some of the melted butter. Place another sheet on
top and brush with the butter. Keep doing this until all the remaining dough
has been done. Cut the stack of dough, lengthwise into 6 strips. Place in a
damp cloth. For each triangle of dough, add 1 tablespoon of the filling. Fold the
end over the filling to form a triangle. Repeat until all the dough has been used.
Place on a baking sheet and brush with the butter. Bake in a preheated 375
degrees F. oven for 18 to 20 minutes. Makes 48.

ROAST BEEF WITH BLUE CHEESE MARINADE

Meat:

A six pound roast will serve 8 people.

Marinade:

1-4 oz. package blue cheese
½ C. fresh lemon juice
3 T. flour
3 dashes of Tabasco sauce
2 cloves garlic, finely chopped

1 T. dried mustard
½ tsp. pepper
½ tsp. salt
1 tsp. Worcestershire sauce
2 tsp. dried onion
1 C. water

Mix all ingredients well, except for the dried onion and water. Make a paste. Cover the meat with the paste. Cover and refrigerate for 2 days. When ready to serve, place meat in a roasting pan. Sprinkle the roast with 2 teaspoons of dried onion and add the water to the roasting pan. Bake in a preheated 300 degrees F. oven for 3 hours. Stain the liquid for the gravy. This is enough marinade to cover a six pound roast.

BAKED HAM WITH CHAMPAGNE SAUCE

1-10 lb. ham

1 bottle champagne
Maple syrup

The day before you are to serve the ham, pour the champagne over the ham. Cover and refrigerate. Baste the ham with the champagne before baking. Bake in a preheated 350 degrees F. oven. Allow 20 minutes per pound. Baste every 30 minutes with the champagne. One hour before finishing, rub with the maple syrup. Baste with the champagne one last time. Serves 8.

BIBB LETTUCE WITH BLUE CHEESE DRESSING

4 heads bib lettuce
1 C. mayonnaise
½ C. plain low-fat yogurt

2 T. tarragon vinegar
1 C. crumbled blue cheese
3 T. thinly sliced scallions
Salt and fresh ground pepper

Rinse the lettuce and dry. Combine the mayonnaise and yogurt and blend until smooth. Add the rest of the ingredients. Pour over the lettuce and toss. Serves 6 to 8. You can make the dressing and refrigerate for a week before serving.

ARTICHOKE MUSHROOM SALAD

4 –14 oz. cans artichoke bottoms
4 heads of Boston lettuce

1 lb. white mushrooms, sliced
1 bunch watercress, leaves only
Paprika

Drain the artichoke bottoms. Tear the lettuce into bit size pieces. Add all the ingredients together.

Dressing:

2 C. sour cream
2 tsp. dry mustard

2 T. fresh lemon juice
½ tsp. salt
½ tsp. fresh ground pepper

Mix all the ingredients together and refrigerate. When ready to use, pour over the salad. Serves 24.

CHAMPAGNE FRUIT SALAD

1 pineapple, peeled, corded and cut into
   bite size pieces
1 cantaloupe, peeled and cut in bite
   size pieces
½ watermelon, seeded and cut up

½ lb. grapes
½ lb. black cherries, sliced in half
3 bananas, sliced
½ lb. strawberries, sliced in half

Layer the fruit in a serving bowl. Make sure the strawberries are on the top.

Dressing:

1 T. olive oil
1 tsp. tarragon vinegar
1 T. sherry

1 T. brandy
½ tsp. tarragon

Mix all the ingredients and pour over the fruit. Cover and refrigerate until ready
to serve.

½ pt. champagne

1 oz. pistachio nuts

Pour the champagne over the fruit when ready to serve. Sprinkle the nuts over
the fruit. Serves 8.

BABY LIMA BEANS

2-20 oz. pkg. frozen baby lima beans
1 stick butter
2 leeks, white parts only

7 strips bacon, crisply cooked and
   crumbled
Salt and pepper to taste

Finely slice the leeks. In a frying pan, melt the butter. Add the leeks and cook
over medium heat for 6 minutes. Bring a pan with salted water to a boil and
add the beans. Cover and cook for 6 minutes. Drain. Place in a bowl and add
the leeks, bacon, salt and pepper. Toss and serve. Serves 12.

SWEET POTATO BALLS

3 sweet potatoes, peeled and quartered
½ tsp. salt
½ tsp. nutmeg
1 egg, beaten

1 ¾ C. finely chopped pecans
¼ C. butter, melted
½ C. brown sugar
3 T. corn syrup

Boil potatoes, until tender. Drain and mash. Stir in salt and nutmeg and shape into 2-inch balls. Dip in the egg and roll in the pecans. Place in a 6 ½ x10x2-inch dish. In the melted butter, add the brown sugar and syrup. Pour over the potatoes. Cook in a preheated 350 degrees F. oven until hot. Makes 6 servings.

WILD RICE CASSEROLE

4 oz. uncooked wild rice
3 C. water
2 T. butter
½ lb. fresh mushrooms, chopped
1 green pepper, chopped
2 onions, chopped

2 C. tomato juice
½ C. chopped fresh parsley
½ tsp. thyme
1 tsp. salt
¼ tsp. paprika
1 C. cheddar cheese, grated

Cook the rice in boiling water for 20 minutes and drain. Saute mushrooms, pepper and onion in the butter for 5 minutes. Add the tomato juice and cook for 10 minutes. Remove and add the parsley and seasonings. In a buttered casserole, make layers of rice, mushroom mixture and cheese. Bake in preheated 350 degrees F. oven for 45 minutes. Serves 6.

CHOCOLATE COVERED STRAWBERRIES

2 pints strawberries (about 32)   1 lb. semisweet chocolate

Melt the chocolate over a double broiler. Holding the strawberries by its stem, dip them into the chocolate. Place on a baking sheet lined with wax paper. Refrigerate at least 20 minutes.

ITALIAN CREAM WEDDING CAKE

¾ lb. butter
1 ½ C. canola oil
6 C. sugar
15 eggs, separated
3 C. buttermilk

3 tsp. baking soda
6 C. flour
3 tsp. vanilla
3 C. coconut
1 ½ C. pecans, roasted and chopped

Beat egg whites until stiff peaks form. Set aside. Cream butter, oil and sugar until fluffy. Add egg yolks one at a time, beating after each one with an electric beater. Stir the soda in the buttermilk. Set aside. Add flour into the butter mixture, alternating with the buttermilk. Add the vanilla, coconut and nuts. Fold the egg whites into the batter. Pour into greased and parchment lined 3-tier pans. Bake in a preheated 325 degrees F. oven for 40 minutes. Cool and frost.

Frosting:

4 C. powdered sugar
2-8 oz. cream cheese, softened

1 stick unsalted butter, softened
4 tsp. vanilla extract

Mix with an electric mixer all ingredients until smooth and creamy. Ice the cake and keep refrigerated until serving time.

SUMMER PICNIC

SODA SANGRIA   SANGRIA

JALAPENO CHEESE DIP WITH CHIPS

CORNISH HENS

BAKED POTATO SALAD

SWEET AND SOUR BEANS

FRENCH BREAD

CHOCOLATE CHIP COOKIES   FRESH FRUIT

"THE COURSE OF NATURE IS
THE ART OF GOD."
EDWARD YOUNG

SODA SANGRIA

1 orange, sliced thin
1 lemon, sliced thin
1 small can frozen lemonade, thawed

1-16 oz. Hawaiian Punch
   concentrate
3 C. water
2-12 oz. cans fresca

Stir together all the ingredients. Serve over ice.

SANGRIA

1 orange, cut in half
¼ C. sugar
2 C. fresh orange juice

1 bottle dry red wine
½ C. Cointreau

Take one half of the orange and cut off the peeling in a spiral shape. In a bowl, place the peeling and sugar. Take a spoon and smash the peel to release the aroma. Add orange juice, wine and Cointreau. Stir. Cover and chill. After 15 minutes remove the peel. Serve over ice and add orange slices. Make 9 servings.

JALAPENO CHEESE DIP

Judy McLean, Albuquerque, NM.

2-8 oz. cream cheese
½ onion, chopped
½ bell pepper, chopped
3 or 4 jalapenos, chopped

1 tsp. garlic salt
1 tsp. Worstershire sauce
1 tsp. lemon juice
1 C. pecans, chopped

Soften the cream cheese. You can chop the onion, pepper and jalapenos in a food processor. Mix all ingredients together. Refrigerate to set.

CORNISH HENS

Cornish hens, 1 per person
Salt and pepper
Dijon mustard
White unseasoned breadcrumbs

Minced shallots
Butter
White wine

Rub each bird with the salt, pepper and 1 tablespoon mustard. Sprinkle with the breadcrumbs. Wrap each hen in foil. Add 1 teaspoon minced shallots, 1 tablespoon butter and 3 tablespoons wine to each hen. Seal. Bake in a preheated 400 degrees F. oven for 45 minutes. Open the foil and bake 15 more minutes. Seal and carry to the picnic.

BAKED POTATO SALAD

5 potatoes, baked
1 C. red onion, chopped
1 ½ C. celery, chopped
1 C. cooked bacon, chopped
½ C. cheddar cheese, grated
1 ½ C. Monterey Jack cheese, grated

1 C. sour cream
3 C. ranch dressing
1 tsp. pepper
1 tsp. celery salt
1 tsp. garlic salt
¼ C. fresh parsley, chopped
Salt to taste

Let potatoes cool for 3 to 4 hours. Peel and dice into chunks. In a large bowl, add the onion, celery, bacon and cheeses. Mix well. In a separate bowl, combine the sour cream, ranch dressing, pepper, celery salt, garlic salt and fresh parsley. Stir well and add to potato mixture. Add salt if needed. Cover and refrigerate for 3 to 4 hours. Makes 12 to 14 servings.

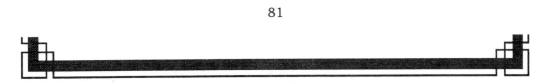

SWEET AND SOUR BEANS

Carol Adams, Fort Stockton, TX.

1 C. sugar	1 T. garlic salt
1 C. vinegar	2 to 3 cans whole green beans,
1 C. oil	drained

Mix all together first 4 ingredients. Pour over green beans. Refrigerate at least 24 hours. Drain and serve. Serves 8 to 10.

CHOCOLATE CHIP COOKIES

Ilene Pylman, Scottsdale, AZ.

1 C. butter	2 tsp. vanilla
1/3 C. margarine	3 ½ C. sifted flour, more if needed
1 C. sugar	1 tsp. baking soda
1 C. packed brown sugar	1 tsp. salt
2 eggs	1-12 oz. semi-sweet chocolate chips

Mix butter, margarine, sugars, eggs and vanilla thoroughly. Add flour, soda and salt. Mix well and stir in chips. Drop by the teaspoonful (in a mound) onto a greased cookie sheet. Bake in a preheated 375 degrees F. oven for 7 ½ to 8 minutes. Remove from oven even if they don't appear done. Makes 5 dozen cookies.

LADIES LUNCHEON

PINEAPPLE TEA

APRICOT AND CHAMPAGNE DRINK

ASPARAGUS WRAPS

CHICKEN AND RASPBERRY SALAD

CHEESE BREAD

KEY LIME PIE

"ONE IS NOT BORN A WOMAN-
ONE BECOMES ONE."
SIMONE de BEAUVOIR

PINEAPPLE TEA

2 T. unsweetened instant tea
1 C. sugar
2 C. boiling water
4 C. unsweetened pineapple juice

1 ½ C. cold water
½ C. fresh lemon juice
Maraschino cherries
Pineapple chunks

In two ice trays, fill ¼ full and freeze. When frozen place the cherries on top of one ice tray and the other one place the pineapple chunks. Fill with water and refreeze. Stir the tea and sugar together. Pour the boiling water over the tea mixture and stir until it is dissolved. Add the pineapple juice, cold water and lemon juice to the mixture. Chill. When ready to serve, place the ice cubes in glasses and pour the tea over. Serves 8.

APRICOT AND CHAMPAGNE DRINK

1-750 ml bottle brut champagne, chilled
2 ½ C. apricot nectar, chilled

3 T. Grand Marnier

Mix all together. Pour into champagne flutes. Serves 8.

ASPARAGUS WRAPS

6 oz. blue cheese, crumbled
1-8 oz. cream cheese, softened
1 egg

1 lb. loaf white bread, crust removed
1-10 oz. pkg. frozen asparagus
½ C. butter, melted

Mix the blue cheese, cream cheese and egg. Flatten each piece with a rolling pin. Spread the mixture on each piece and add 1 piece of the asparagus on each. Roll the slices. Place in freezer and freeze at least 4 hours. When ready to serve, place on a baking sheet and brush with the butter. Bake in a preheated 350 degrees F. oven and bake for 10 minutes. Cut into bite-size pieces. Makes 10 servings.

CHICKEN AND RASPBERRY SALAD

Raspberry Wine Vinegar:

3 C. fresh or frozen raspberries   1 C. sugar
2-17 oz. bottles white wine vinegar

In a saucepan, combine all the ingredients and bring to a boil. Cover, reduce the heat, and simmer for 10 minutes. Stain through a strainer. Place in a jar and cover. Store in the refrigerator. Makes 5 cups.

Marinade:

¼ C. dried mustard   1 ½ tsp. olive oil
2 T. brown sugar   2 cloves garlic, minced
3 T. water   Pepper to taste
1 T. raspberry wine vinegar

Combine all the ingredients.

4 boneless chicken breasts, halved

Place in a shallow dish, and pour the marinade over. Refrigerate for 2 hours. Place on a greased baking sheet and broil 5 minutes on each side. Cut chicken into strips and set aside.

Salad Dressing:

¼ C. oil free salad dressing   ¼ C. raspberry wine vinegar

Mix together and pour over assorted salad greens. Add the chicken and toss. Add fresh or frozen raspberries, thawed, on top.

CHEESE BREAD

1-16 oz. loaf frozen white bread dough
1 tsp. dried oregano, crushed
½ tsp. garlic salt

½ tsp. paprika
¼ tsp. celery seed
¼ tsp. onion powder
2 C. cheddar cheese, shredded

Thaw the bread. On a floured surface, roll the bread dough into a 15x10x1-inch rectangle. Place the dough in a greased pan and cover. Let rise in a warm place for 1½ hours or until doubled. Combine the rest of the ingredients and sprinkle over the bread dough. Bake in a preheated 375 degrees F. oven for 20 minutes or until golden brown. Cool. Cut into serving size pieces. Makes 30 pieces.

KEY LIME PIE

9-inch pie crust, baked
1½ C. sugar
1½ key limes, juiced
Grate of 1 key lime

3 eggs
2 T. cornstarch
2 T. flour
2 C. milk
1 T. butter

Mix all ingredients in a double boiler. Stirring constantly until thick. This takes about 20 to 25 minutes. Pour into the pie crust. You can add a meringue or add a spoonful of whipping cream to each slice. Garnish with a lime slice.

FOURTH OF JULY CELEBRATION

WATERMELON PUNCH   WATERMELON DAIQUIRIS

SPINACH TORTILLA ROLL UPS   CHILLED PEA SOUP

GRILLED SALMON STEAKS TERIYAKI

HAWAIIAN FRUIT SALAD

SOUR CREAM SUMMER SQUASH

GRILLED CORN WITH BASIL BUTTER

PARMESAN BREAD

CHEESECAKE ICE CREAM   ICEBOX SUGAR COOKIES

"A NATION IS A BODY OF PEOPLE WHO
HAVE DONE GREAT THINGS TOGETHER."
ERNEST REMAN

WATERMELON PUNCH

½ C. sugar
½ C. water
½ of 6 ¼ oz. can frozen pink
  lemonade, thawed

½ large watermelon,
  cut lengthwise
3 C. melon balls
1-28 oz. bottle ginger ale, chilled

Combine sugar with the water. Boil for five minutes. Add lemonade and chill. Clean out the watermelon half and make your melon balls. You will be using the watermelon half to serve the punch from. Pour punch into the hollowed out shell, add melon balls and ginger ale. Makes about a dozen drinks.

WATERMELON DAIQUIRI

4 C. seeded and cubed
  watermelon
½ C. light rum

¼ C. fresh lime juice
¼ C. orange-flavored liqueur
Ice cubes

Freeze watermelon in a shallow pan at least 6 hours. Combine frozen watermelon, rum, lime juice and liqueur in an electric blender. Mix until smooth. Add enough ice to bring mixture to 5-cup level. Mix until smooth.

CHILLED PEA SOUP

10 oz. pkg. frozen peas
1 C. condensed chicken broth
1 C. light cream
1 stalk celery, chopped

1large lettuce leaf, chopped
1 T. chopped onion
Salt and pepper to taste

Cook peas as directed on package. Cool. Place all ingredients in a blender. Cover and blend until smooth. Chill thoroughly. Garnish each serving with snipped parsley . Serve in frosted wine glasses. Serves 4.

SPINACH TORTILLA ROLLS

Carol Adams, Fort Stockton, TX.

1 pkg. frozen spinach, drained
6 slices cooked and crumbled bacon
¼ C. mayonnaise
4 oz. cream cheese

½ C. chopped green onions
1 tsp. salt
½ tsp. pepper
Flour tortillas

Mix together all ingredients, except tortillas. Spread mixture on the flour tortillas. Roll up the tortillas and chill. Cut 1-inch slices and place on a cookie sheet. Bake in a preheated 400 degrees F. oven for 7 minutes. Serve hot.

GRILLED SALMON STEAKS TERIYAKI

4 salmon steaks,
  approximately ½ inch thick
½ tsp. sesame oil
4 tsp. soy sauce

2 tsp. lemon juice
1 garlic clove, minced
Salt and pepper to taste
1 T. butter, melted

Place steaks in a shallow pan. Mix remaining ingredients, except butter. Pour over salmon. Let stand twenty minutes at room temperature, turning occasionally. Remove steaks from marinade. Brush both sides with melted butter and grill 5 to 7 minutes on each side, until browned and easily flaked. Serves 4.

HAWAIIAN FRUIT SALAD

Fresh pineapple, split lengthwise
Fresh fruit of your choosing

Champagne or orange liqueur
Poppy seed dressing

Scoop out pineapple and chop the fruit. Add the pineapple to the fresh fruit of your choice and marinate the fruits in champagne or the orange liqueur until chilled. Drain. Fill the pineapple halves with the fruit and pour on a little of the poppy seed dressing.

Poppy Seed Dressing:

¼ C. honey
3 T. cider vinegar
2 T. olive oil
1 small shallot, minced

2 tsp. Dijon mustard
1 tsp. poppy seeds
Salt and pepper to taste

Whisk together all the ingredients in a small bowl or shake in a jar until smooth. Cover and refrigerate. Makes about 2/3 cups.

SOUR CREAM SUMMER SQUASH

1 large summer squash
2 T. vinegar
1 tsp. salt
2 tsp. butter

2 tsp. finely snipped dill
½ tsp. paprika
2 tsp. chopped chives
¼ C. sour cream

Peel and slice squash into ¼-inch strips. Mix with vinegar and salt. Let stand for 30 minutes. Drain thoroughly. Simmer squash in butter until tender but not soft, about 5 minutes. Stir in dill, chives and paprika. Add sour cream gradually. Do not boil. Serves 6 to 8.

GRILLED FRESH CORN WITH BASIL BUTTER

8 ears fresh corn, husked
Softened butter

1/3 C. finely chopped basil
Salt and pepper to taste

Place 1 ear of corn on each of 8 heavy-duty foil sheets large enough to wrap around them. Spread the butter on ear of corn, covering all sides. Sprinkle evenly with the basil, salt and pepper. Add a few drops of water to each packet and wrap securely. Place the corn packets on the grill for about 10 minutes, turning the packet 3 times. Serves 8.

PARMESAN BREAD

1 loaf French bread   ½ C. grated Parmesan cheese
½ lb. butter, melted   2 T. fresh parsley, minced

Slice bread diagonally to, but not through, the bottom crust. Combine butter, cheese and parsley. Spread the mixture on sides of each slice. Wrap in foil and heat on the grill or oven.

CHEESECAKE ICE CREAM

3-8 oz. pkg. cream cheese,   5 eggs
  room temperature   2 T. lemon juice
2 ½ C. sugar   2 tsp. vanilla
                                        5 C. light cream

With an electric mixer, beat the cream cheese and sugar until smooth. Beat in the eggs, lemon juice and vanilla till smooth. Stir in the cream. Freeze in a 4 or 5 qt. ice cream freezer. Makes 3 qts.

ICEBOX SUGAR COOKIES

1 ½ C. flour
1 ½ tsp. baking powder
¼ tsp. salt
1 ¼ sticks unsalted butter,
    softened

2/3 C. sugar
1 large egg
2 tsp. vanilla
¼ tsp. finely grated lemon zest

Whisk first 3 ingredients thoroughly. Beat on medium speed with an electric mixer the next 2 ingredients until very fluffy and well blended. Add the next three ingredients and beat until well combined. Stir the flour mixture into the butter mixture until well blended and smooth. Cover and refrigerate until slightly firm, 30 minutes. Place the dough on one end of a long sheet of wax paper. With lightly greased hands, shape into an even, 11-inch-long log. You can store in the refrigerator for up to 1 mouth. When ready to bake, slice into 1/8-inch-thick slices. Place on a greased cookie sheet. Preheat oven to 375 degrees F. Bake 7 to 10 minutes. Take out and place on a rack. This makes 3 ½ to 4 dozen cookies.

NOTES

SUMMER BARBEQUE

NON-ALCOHOLIC SLUSH   RUM SLUSH

GRILLED QUESADILLAS

FRUIT WITH RUM SAUCE

BARBEQUE BRISKET   CAJUN GRILLED SHRIMP

CAESAR SALAD

GRILLED FRESH CORN

BILLY'S POTATO CASSEROLE

GARLIC FRENCH BREAD

STRAWBERRY SORBET   PECAN CRISPS

"A FRIEND IS ONE BEFORE WHOM I MAY THINK ALOUD."
RALPH WALDO EMERSON

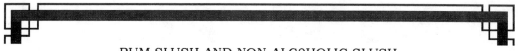

RUM SLUSH AND NON-ALCOHOLIC SLUSH

1 pkg. strawberry Kool-Aid
  (no sugar)
1 qt. water
2-12 oz. frozen orange juice
  (unsweetened)

3 cans water
2 large cans unsweetened
  pineapple juice
Fifth of rum
Diet 7-Up

Mix all ingredients, except 7-Up, in a large container and freeze. When ready to serve, fill cup halfway with the slush and pour the Diet 7-Up over. This is great drink for a very hot day.

To make the nonalcoholic drink, omit the rum.

GRILLED QUESADILLAS

12 scallions
8 flour tortillas

¼ lb. Monterey Jack cheese, grated
1 jalapeno pepper, minced
½ C. cilantro leaves

Brush scallions with oil and grill 1 to 2 minutes. Set aside. Brush one side of a tortilla with oil. Place oil-side down on a plate. Sprinkle a quarter of the cheese, jalapeno and cilantro on the tortilla. Arrange 3 scallions on top. Top with another tortilla. Place onto grill. Brush top of the tortilla with oil. When underside is brown and cheese melts, flip over and grill other side. Cut quesadillas into wedges with a knife. Serve immediately. Serves 8.

RUM SAUCE FOR FRUIT

2 C. sour cream
½ C. brown sugar

1 T. vanilla
1 T. dark rum

Place the sour cream into medium bowl. Whisk the sour cream and brown sugar until the mixture is blended and fairly smooth. It won't be completely smooth at this point. Add vanilla into the sour cream. Whisk. Pour the rum into it. Whisk until the sauce is very smooth. Cover with plastic wrap. Keep the sauce in the refrigerator until ready to serve. The sauce is better if made the day before. Makes about 2 ¼ cups. Set the sauce out and let everyone dip the fruit into it.

BARBEQUE BRISKET

1 large brisket, trimmed
2 T. Worcestershire sauce
Celery salt
Onion salt
Garlic salt

Salt and pepper
3 oz. liquid smoke
1 bottle of your favorite barbeque
sauce

In the morning before the day you will be serving the brisket, add ingredients to brisket, except barbeque sauce. Wrap in foil and refrigerate all day. Before going to bed, place the brisket in oven at 225 degrees F. Take out of the oven when you get up the next morning. One hour before serving, add barbeque sauce and cook at 350 degrees F. for 1 hour. Serve immediately. To determine the serving amount, allow ½ lb. per person.

CAJUN GRILLED SHRIMP

Cajun Marinade:

1 C. vegetable oil
¼ C. Worcestershire sauce
½ C. dry red wine
½ C. dark soy sauce
¼ C. red wine vinegar

½ C. lemon juice
2 T. dry mustard
4 cloves garlic, pressed
½ C. parsley, finely cut
Salt, pepper, cayenne & white
    pepper

Place uncooked, peeled and deveined shrimp in a large glass bowl. Combine marinade ingredients and pour over shrimp. Cover and refrigerate 2 hours. Preheat grill. Place shrimp onto bamboo skewers. Pour reserved marinade into small saucepan. Bring to boil. Reduce heat and simmer for 5 minutes. Grill shrimp just until they turn pink, turning once. They cook in a few minutes. Serve hot with reserved marinade for dipping. To determine the serving amount, allow 1/3 lb. per person.

CAESAR SALAD

3 heads romaine lettuce
1 head chicory
2 C. bread cubes, unseasoned
¾ C. olive oil
3 cloves garlic, crushed

2 eggs, at room temperature
1 T. lemon juice
1 T. red wine vinegar
1 t. salt
½ t. freshly ground pepper
4 T. freshly grated Parmesan cheese

Tear the lettuce into large bite-size pieces. Refrigerate for a least 1 hour. To make the croutons, heat ¼ cup of the olive oil in a heavy skillet. Add the crushed garlic cloves and sauté until golden. Remove and discard the garlic. Take off the heat and add the bread cubes, stirring rapidly with a fork to coat all sides. Turn the heat to low, place skillet over heat and continue stirring until the cubes are browned evenly. Drain on a paper towel.
Set aside uncovered. Just before serving, place greens in a bowl. Add the remaining ½ cup oil and toss lightly to coat the greens. Lower the eggs in the shell in boiling water and cook 1 minute only. Cool under cold running water. Break the eggs directly over the greens. Add the lemon juice, vinegar, salt and pepper. Toss again. Add the grated Parmesan cheese and toss. Add the croutons just before serving. Serve immediately. Serves 10.

GRILLED FRESH CORN

Strip the husks down, but do not tear them off. Remove the silk completely and replace the husks over the corn, tying with string at the top of the ear. Roast over a hot fire for about 20 minutes, turning 2 to 3 times. Allow 2 ears per person.

BILLY'S POTATO CASSEROLE

Billy McLean, Albuquerque, NM.

½ chopped bell pepper
½ chopped onion
8 medium potatoes, peeled and
    sliced thin
8 oz. can of chopped green chilies

1 can cream of mushroom soup
1 C. milk
6 slices crisp cooked bacon,
    crumbled
1 pkg. Durkee's cheese sauce

Saute the bell pepper and onion in butter until soft. Combine the rest of the ingredients with the pepper and onions. Place in a 9x13-inch baking dish and cover. Bake in preheated 350 degrees F. oven for 1½ hours. Serves 8.

GARLIC FRENCH BREAD

1 loaf French bread
1 clove of garlic, pressed
6 T. of butter

¼ t. lemon juice
¼ t. cracked black pepper

Slice the loaf diagonally into ¾-inch slices without cutting through the bottom crust. Add the rest of ingredients and spread on each slice. Wrap tightly in foil and heat 20 minutes in a preheated 350 degrees F oven. You can make this up before hand and freeze before baking.

STRAWBERRY SORBET

1 pkg. frozen strawberry, thawed   1 t. sugar
3 T. Framboise liqueur

Place strawberries in a blender. Add the Framboise liqueur and sugar. Blend until smooth. Pour into a container and freeze. Serve in parfait glasses. Makes about 1 pint.

PECAN CRISPS

1 ¼ C. chopped pecans	½ C. packed light brown sugar
2 1/3 C. flour	½ C. powdered sugar
½ t. baking soda	1 large egg
½ t. salt	½ C. vegetable oil
1 stick unsalted butter, softened	1 t. vanilla extract

Spread pecans in a single layer in a large baking pan and toast in the oven for 7 to 8 minutes, stirring occasionally, until browned. Remove from the oven and set-aside until cool. Thoroughly stir together flour, baking soda and salt. In a large mixing bowl, combine butter, brown and powdered sugars, and beat until fluffy and smooth. Add egg. oil and vanilla and beat until well mixed. Beat in dry ingredients. Stir in half of toasted, cooled pecans. Cover and refrigerate dough for 1 hour. Divide dough in half. Lay each half on a 15-inch long sheet of waxed paper and shape into smooth 2-inch diameter logs about 9 ½-inches long. Sprinkle half of remaining pecans over each log, pressing and patting them into the surface. Wrap tightly and freeze for at least 4 hours, or until very firm. These can be frozen up to 2 weeks. Preheat the oven to 375 degrees F. Grease several baking sheets. Remove from freezer, cut quickly into ¼-inch-thick slices, and place 1 ½ inches apart on baking sheets. Place in upper third of the oven and bake for 9 to 11 minutes, or until nicely colored all over and slightly darker around edges. Cool on a wire rack. Makes 55 to 60.

NOTES

LABOR DAY CELEBRATION

MANGO SMOOTHIE   APRICOT SLUSH

GREEN CHILI AND ARTICHOKE DIP

GRILLED SPICY CHICKEN

BLACK BEAN AND CORN SALAD

SCALLOPED NEW POTATOES WITH SPINACH

FRIED OKRA WITH JALAPENOS

GRILLED FRENCH BREAD

WHITE CHOCOLATE SNICKERS CHEESECAKE

"WORK IS NOT MAN'S PUNISHMENT, IT IS
HIS REWARD AND HIS STRENGTH, HIS GLORY
AND HIS PLEASURE."
GEORGE SAND

MANGO SMOOTHIE

2 C. diced ripe mango
2 C. water

2 T. sugar
2 T. fresh lime juice

Combine all ingredients in a blender and blend until smooth. Add water if needed to thin the drink to pour. Pour into tall glasses over ice. Serves 4.

APRICOT SLUSH

1-46 oz. can apricot nectar
1-46 oz. can unsweetened pineapple
  juice
1-6 oz. can frozen orange juice, thawed

1-6 oz. can frozen lemonade
  concentrate, thawed
1 C. vodka
1 C. apricot brandy
2 bottles lemon-lime sodas, chilled

Combine all the ingredients, except the lemon-lime sodas, in a 4-quart plastic container and freeze. To serve, spoon 1 cup frozen mixture into each glass and pour the lemon-line soda over. Makes 16 servings.

GREEN CHILI AND ARTICHOKE DIP

1 can artichoke hearts
7 oz. green chilies

1 C. mayonnaise
1 C. shredded Parmesan cheese

Chop artichokes and mix all the ingredients. Bake in a preheated 350 degrees F. oven for 30 minutes. Jalapenos may be added. Serves 8 to 10.

GRILLED SPICY CHICKEN

6 chicken breasts, skinned
½ C. fresh lime juice
¼ C. honey
2 T. fresh cilantro leaves
3 cloves garlic, chopped

2 jalapeno peppers, unseeded and
   sliced
2 T. soy sauce
½ tsp. salt
½ tsp. pepper

Combine all ingredients in a blender, except the chicken, and blend until smooth. Place chicken in 13x9x2-inch dish and pour all but ¼ cup of the marinade over the chicken. Cover and refrigerate for 8 hours. When ready to cook, place a pan of water with a wire rack in the water and place on the grill. Drain the chicken and place on the rack. Cook for 30 minutes. Turn the chicken and brush on the marinade. Cook for 30 more minutes. Serves 6.

BLACK BEAN AND CORN SALAD

1-15 oz. can whole kernel sweet corn,
   drained
1-15 oz. can black beans, drained
½ C. green onions, chopped
2 cloves garlic, minced
¼ C. fresh cilantro, chopped

¼ tsp. red pepper
4 large tomatoes
½ C. Italian dressing
½ tsp. salt
fresh ground pepper

Cut tomatoes in half. Remove the centers and chop well. Turn the tomato shells upside down and drain on paper towels. Set aside. Add the chopped up tomatoes to the corn, beans, onion, garlic, cilantro and red pepper. Add the Italian dressing. Toss well. Add the salt and pepper. Cover mixture and refrigerate for 3 to 4 hours. Also refrigerate the tomato halves. When ready to serve, spoon the mixture in the tomatoes. Serves 4.

SCALLOPED NEW POTATOES WITH SPINACH

2 lb. new potatoes, sliced
3 T. butter
1 onion, chopped
3 cloves garlic, minced
3 T. flour
1 tsp. dried rosemary
1 tsp. dried parsley

½ tsp. salt
½ tsp. pepper
1 ¾ C. milk
6 C. torn spinach
1 red pepper, cut in strips
1 C. white cheddar cheese, grated
¼ C. dry unseasoned bread crumbs,
   finely crumbled

Cook potatoes in water until just tender, about 5 minutes. Place in a large bowl. In a heavy frying pan over medium heat, melt 2 tablespoons of the butter. Add the onion and garlic and cook 5 minutes until tender. Stir in flour, rosemary, parsley, salt and pepper. Stir in the milk and cook over medium heat until thick and bubbly. Add the spinach and red pepper to the potatoes. Mix well. Pour the sauce over the potato mixture and mix. Place mixture in a baking dish. Over medium heat melt the 1 tablespoon of butter and cook the breadcrumbs until coated. Sprinkle the cheese and bread crumbs over the potatoes. Bake in preheated 375 degrees F. oven for 20 minutes. Serves 12.

FRIED OKRA WITH JALAPENOS

1 lb. fresh okra, sliced
1 large green tomato, diced
1 onion, chopped
1 clove garlic, minced
1 jalapeno pepper, halved and sliced

3 eggs, beaten
½ tsp. salt
¼ tsp. pepper
½ C. milk
1 C. cornmeal
¼ C. vegetable oil

Combine the first 5 ingredients and mix. Set aside. In a bowl combine eggs, salt, pepper and milk. Pour over the okra mixture and coat. Add the cornmeal and mix well. Heat the oil in a skillet over medium heat until hot. Add the okra and reduce heat to medium low. Cover and fry until golden brown. This takes about 10 to 15 minutes. Invert on a plate and slide other side up into the skillet and cook uncovered for 5 to 8 minutes. Remove from the skillet and drain on paper towels. Serves 6.

GRILLED FRENCH BREAD

1 loaf French bread
1 stick unsalted butter, softened
3 cloves garlic, minced

½ C. fresh cilantro, minced
½ tsp. salt
¼ tsp. pepper

Cut the bread diagonally into ¾ -inch slices. Cream the butter with a whisk in a mixing bowl. Add the rest of the ingredients. Mix well. Brush on the bread slices and place on the grill, until brown. Turn over and brown the other sides. Makes 20 to 24 slices.

WHITE CHOCOLATE SNICKERS CHEESECAKE

Pat Snyder, Dallas, TX.

Crust:

2/3 C. graham cracker crumbs
2/3 C. sugar
1 tsp. cinnamon

3 T. unsalted butter, softened
6 snicker bars, chilled and finely
chopped

Mix all the ingredients together, except the snicker bars. Wrap the outside of a 10-inch spring form pan with 2 layers of foil. You will be baking the cheesecake in a pan of water and you do not want the water to seep through. Place the crumb mixture in the bottom of the pan. Place half of the snickers in the pan, evenly spread.

Filling:

4-8 oz. pkg. cream cheese, softened
2/3 C. sugar
3 eggs

1 tsp. vanilla
6 oz. white chocolate, melted
¾ C. heavy whipping cream

Beat the cream cheese for 5 minutes with an electric mixer. Add sugar and mix well. Add eggs, one at a time, beating after each egg. Add vanilla and blend well. Add the melted chocolate and cream and mix well. Pour into crust. Place in a pan filled with ½ -inch water. In a preheated 350 degrees F. oven, bake for 1½ hours. Let cool for 2 hours before cutting. Top with the fudge sauce and remaining snickers.

Fudge Sauce:

1 stick unsalted butter
4 oz. unsweetened chocolate
¼ salt

3 C. sugar
1 2/3 C. evaporated milk
1 T. vanilla

Melt the butter and chocolate in a pan over low heat. Add the remaining ingredients until smooth. Whisk for 1 minute. Drizzle over the cheesecake. Serves 12.

BACK TO SCHOOL PARTY

FRESH LEMONADE   SODAS

CHILI CON QUESCO DIP WITH CHIPS

INDIVIDUAL PIZZAS

FRUIT SALAD

ICE CREAM SLICES

"IF YOU THINK EDUCATION IS
EXPENSIVE-TRY IGNORANCE."
DERSK BOK

LEMONADE

3 lemons   3 ½ C. water, boiled
½ C. sugar

Peel the lemon in a spiral. Add the lemon peels, sugar and boiling water. Stir
until sugar is dissolved. Pour into a pitcher. Juice the lemons and remove the
seeds. Add to the pitcher. Stir. Cool. Pour over a glass with ice. Serves 6.

CHILI CON QUESCO

½ C. chopped onion   1 C. American cheese, grated
1 T. oleo   1 C. Monterey Jack cheese, grated
2 tomatoes, chopped   1 tsp. cornstarch
2-4 oz. can chopped green chili   1 tsp. hot pepper sauce
    peppers, drained

In a pan, melt the oleo and cook the onions until tender. Stir in the tomatoes
and peppers. Simmer, 10 minutes. Stir the cornstarch with the cheeses. Add
to the onions, stirring until melted. Stir in the hot sauce. Heat. Serve with
chips. Serves 14.

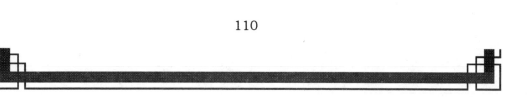

INDIVIDUAL PIZZAS

Dough:

1 1/3 C. lukewarm water	¼ C. olive oil
1 ½ pkg. dry yeast	1 tsp. salt
1 ½ T. honey	5 C. flour

Mix ½ tablespoon honey and 1/3 cup water in large bowl. Add the yeast. Stir
well and set aside, about 10 minutes. Add the honey, olive oil, salt, 1
tablespoon of the honey and remaining water. Mix well with a wooden spoon.
Stir the flour in gradually, stirring often. Turn the dough out onto a floured
surface and knead 10 minutes. Cover the dough with plastic wrap and set aside
for 15 minutes. Separate the dough into 8 pieces. Roll each piece into a ball.
Cover again and let rise for 1 hour. Flatten each piece into a 6-inch circle,
shaping a slightly raised edge. Grease two large cookie sheets and dust the
baking sheets with corn meal. Place the dough on them. Two pizzas will fit on
each baking dish.

Sauce:

3 T. olive oil	2 T. fresh basil, chopped
2 garlic cloves, minced	1 tsp. salt
1 C. canned plum tomatoes, drained	¼ tsp. pepper
1 C. canned plum tomatoes with juice	2 tsp. dried oregano
	1 t. thyme

In a skillet, sauté the garlic and olive oil for 1 minute. Add rest of ingredients
and simmer for 10 minutes. Spread on the pizza dough.

Topping:

1 ¼ lb. mozzarella cheese	½ lb. sliced pepperoni
4 T. Parmesan cheese	2 T. olive oil

Add the mozzarella, Parmesan and pepperoni to the pizzas.   Drizzle with the
olive oil. Bake in a preheated 450 degrees F. oven for 15 minutes.

FRUIT SALAD

1 large can pineapple chunks
1 large can mandarin oranges

1 C. green seedless grapes
2 bananas, sliced
1 avocado, chopped

Drain the fruits, reserving the liquids. Add all the ingredients together and set aside.

Dressing:

1 C. sugar
1 T. cornstarch

3 T. lemon juice
1 egg, beaten
1 C. pineapple juice

In a saucepan, mix all the ingredients. Cook slowly over medium heat, stirring constantly until thickened. Cool before pouring over the fruit mixture. Chill before serving. Makes 4 to 6 servings.

ICE CREAM PIE SLICES

Crust:

¼ C. pecans, finely chopped

1 C. vanilla wafer crumbs
¼ C. butter, melted

Add all the ingredients together. Press into bottom and sides of a 9-inch glass pie dish. Bake until golden, about 10 minutes.

1 qt. vanilla ice cream, softened

Spread the ice cream into the piecrust. Freeze until firm.

Toppings: Have these setting out for the kids to add their own toppings.

2 large cans whipping cream
1 large can chocolate syrup
1 C. pecan, finely chopped
3 bananas, sliced
1 jar maraschino cherries

NOTES

HALLOWEEN DINNER

HOT SPICED APPLE CIDER   ZOMBIES

ARTICHOKE CHEESE SQUARES

GLAZED PORK ROAST

SPINACH SALAD WITH GRAPEFRUIT,
ORANGE AND AVOCADO

CRUNCHY SQUASH CASSEROLE

BRUSSELS SPROUTS WITH MUSTARD SAUCE

SWEET POTATO BISCUITS

BREAD PUDDING WITH WHISKEY SAUCE

JAMAICAN JAVA

"THE SUSPENSE IS TERRIBLE. I HOPE IT WILL LAST.
OSCAR WILDE

HOT SPICED APPLE CIDER

1 gallon apple cider
1- 9 oz. box of cinnamon red-hot candies
½ C. sugar
5 cinnamon sticks

20 whole cloves
1 C. cranberry juice
1 C. orange juice
Butter

In a large pot, combine all the ingredients except the butter. Over a medium heat, bring to boil. Stir this frequently until sugar and candies are dissolved. Reduce heat and simmer for 1 hour. Before serving, place a small pat of butter in each mug. Garnish with a cinnamon stick in each mug.

ZOMBIES

12 oz. white rum
12 oz. dark rum
4 C. pineapple juice

1 ½ C. orange juice
1 C. lime juice
4 oz. dark rum

Mix all the ingredients, except the last ingredient, in a large pitcher. Stir well. This can be made a day ahead. Pour over ice in a glass and float the rum on top. Serves 8.

ARTICHOKE CHEESE SQUARES

¼ C. onion, chopped
1 clove garlic, mashed
3 T. bacon fat
4 eggs, beaten until frothy
1-14 oz. jar artichoke hearts, drained
  and chopped

½ lb. Swiss cheese, grated
2 T. parsley, minced
½ tsp. salt
¼ tsp. oregano
¼ tsp. Tabasco sauce
½ C. dry unseasoned bread crumbs

In a frying pan sauté onion and garlic in bacon fat. Add the remaining ingredients and mix well. Pour into a greased 7x11-inch baking dish. Bake in a preheated 325 degrees F. oven for 25 to 30 minutes. Cut into 1 inch squares. Makes 77 squares.

GLAZED PORK ROAST

1 8-10 lb. whole loin of pork
Seasoned salt
Paprika
Olive oil

Garlic salt
Pepper
Dry mustard

Rub oil and seasonings all over pork loin and cook in a preheated 400 degrees F. oven for 45 minutes. Turn oven down to 350 degrees F. and cook for another hour. Cover with pork glaze. Serves 16 to 20.

Pork Glaze:

4 green onions, green part only
Grated rind of 1 lemon
Grated rind of 1 orange
2 –25 oz. jars prunes
1 large can pineapple chunks,
    chopped up
 2 sticks butter

½ lb. brown sugar
5 T. Worcestershire sauce
5 T. A-1 sauce
5 T. teriyaki sauce
2/3 C. red wine
1 egg
Salt and pepper to taste

Place all ingredients in a large saucepan and cook over medium heat, until the sauce cooks down, about 45 minutes. Pour over the pork roast.

SPINACH SALAD WITH GRAPEFRUIT, ORANGE, AND AVOCADO

4 T. sesame seeds
6 C. baby spinach leaves
½ tsp. salt
¼ tsp. pepper

5 T. Tangerine Shallot Dressing
1 grapefruit, peeled and sectioned
1 navel orange, peeled and sectioned
1 ripe avocado, peeled and sliced

Toast the sesame seeds briefly in a small skillet over medium heat. Set aside. Toss together in a salad bowl the next 4 ingredients. Divide the spinach among salad plates and arrange on top the next 3 ingredients. Sprinkle with the sesame seeds. Serve immediately. Serve 4.

Tangerine Shallot Dressing:
1 clove garlic, crushed
½ tsp. salt
¼ C. fresh tangerine juice

2 T. fresh lemon juice
3 shallots, minced
¾ C. vegetable oil

Mix the garlic and salt until a paste is formed. Add the tangerine juice, lemon juice and shallots. Whisk until well blended. Add the oil in a slowly, whisking constantly. Use immediately or cover and refrigerate. Makes 1½ cups.

CRUNCHY SQUASH CASSEROLE.

Carol Adams, Fort Stockton, TX.

2-10 oz. frozen slice yellow squash
1 C. chopped onion
1 T. butter
1-8 oz. sour cream
1 can cream of chicken soup

1-8 oz. can water chestnuts, drained
1-6 oz. pkg. chicken flavor stuffing
  mix
¼ C. plus 2 T. butter, melted

Cook squash and drain. Saute onion in the butter. Combine squash, onion, sour cream, soup and water chestnuts. Combine stuffing and the melted butter, stirring well. Add ¾ of stuffing to squash and spoon into a lightly greased casserole. Sprinkle remaining stuffing over casserole. Bake in a preheated 350 degrees F. oven for 20 minutes. Serves 12.

BRUSSELS SPROUTS WITH MUSTARD SAUCE

Carol Adams, Fort Stockton, TX.

1 pkg. frozen Brussels sprouts, cook
  and drain
½ C. cream
¼ C. butter

1 T. Dijon mustard
¼ tsp. salt
Dash Tabasco

Cook all ingredients, except Brussels sprouts, in a pan until thickened. Pour over the brussel sprouts. Serves 4 to 6.

SWEET POTATO BISCUITS

1 large sweet potato
6 T. milk
2 C. flour
1 T. baking powder
1 T. light brown sugar
1 ½ tsp. salt

1/8 tsp. freshly ground pepper
¼ C. chilled unsalted butter,
  cut in bits
2 T. chilled vegetable shortening,
  cut in bits

With a fork, prick the sweet potato, and then cook in a microwave oven for about 7 or 8 minutes, or cook in an oven at 350 degrees F. for 45 minutes. Let cool, then peel and mash with a fork to make 1 cup. Blend the milk in the mashed sweet potato and set aside. You can prepare this 1 day ahead. Cover and refrigerate. When ready to make the biscuits, preheat oven to 425 degrees F. In a large mixing bowl, whisk together the flour, baking powder, brown sugar, salt and pepper. Cut in the butter and shortening until mixture is course. Using a fork, gently beat in the mashed sweet potato mixture to make a soft but manageable dough. Turn dough onto a lightly floured surface and knead about 6 times. Roll or pat to ½ inch thickness and cut with a 2-inch biscuit cutter. Place biscuits about 2 inches apart on a large greased baking sheet. Bake for 15 to 17 minutes. Makes 24 biscuits.

BREAD PUDDING WITH WHISKEY SAUCE

1 loaf French bread
1 qt. milk
4 eggs, well beaten
2 C. sugar

2 T. vanilla extract
1 ½ C. seedless raisins
3 T. margarine, melted
Whiskey sauce

Place the bread in a bowl and cover with the milk, until the bread is soggy. Mix eggs, sugar, vanilla and raisins and stir well. Pour margarine in bottom of an oblong baking pan, and add bread mixture. Pour the egg mixture over the bread. Bake in a preheated 325 degrees F. oven for 45 minutes. Check after 35 minutes. It will be done if it is very firm. When ready to serve, add whiskey sauce and heat under broiler. Makes 8 servings.

Whiskey Sauce:

½ C. butter
1 C. sugar

1 egg, well beaten
Whiskey to taste

Cream butter and sugar and cook in top of a double boiler until very hot and thoroughly dissolved. Add beaten egg and whip rapidly. Let cool and add whiskey. Pour on top of bread pudding.

JAMAICAN JAVA

10 C. freshly brewed hot coffee
10 T. Kahlua

¾ C. heavy cream, whipped
Ground cinnamon

Combine the coffee with the Kahlua. Pour into cups and top each serving with a tablespoon of whipped cream and a sprinkling of cinnamon. Serve immediately. Serves 12.

NOTES

TAIL GATE PARTY

SODAS   TEQUILA SUNRISES   BEER

BLUE CHEESE DIP WITH RAW VEGETABLES

SQUASH SOUP

BARBECUED CHICKEN   TENDER PORK RIBS

POTATO SALAD WITH ARTICHOKE HEARTS

FRENCH BREAD

ICED BROWNIES   FRESH FRUIT

"SPORTS DO NOT BUILD CHARACTER,
THEY REVEAL IT."
HEYWOOD BROUN

123

TEQUILA SUNRISE

6 oz. tequila
16 oz. orange juice

2 oz. grenadine

Fill a glass with ice. Add tequila and fill with the orange juice. Slowly add the grenadine. Serves 4.

BLUE CHEESE DIP WITH RAW VEGETABLES

1-3 oz. cream cheese, softened
½ C. small-curd cottage cheese
2 T. sour cream
¼ tsp. Tabasco sauce
½ tsp. dill
1 clove garlic, crushed

1-1/2 oz. blue cheese dip mix
¼ C. radishes, finely chopped
¼ C. celery, finely chopped
¼ C. green onion, finely chopped
¼ C. green pepper, finely chopped

In a food processor chop all the vegetables. Set aside in bowl. Put cream cheese, cottage cheese and sour cream in the food processor and blend. Add Tabasco sauce, dill, garlic and dip mix. Blend. Stir in chopped vegetables. Refrigerate at least 4 hours before serving. This dip can be kept in the refrigerator for up to 3 days. Serves 8.

SQUASH SOUP

2-10 oz. pkg. frozen squash
2 C. sour cream
2 apples, peeled and cubed
½ tsp. nutmeg
½ tsp. salt

¼ tsp. pepper
2 T. onion, chopped
¼ C. butter
¼ C. flour
4 C. chicken broth
4 cooked bacon slices, crumbled

Cook the squash according to package. In a food processor place sour cream, apples, nutmeg, salt, pepper, onion and ½ of the squash and blend until smooth. Pour in a bowl. Puree remaining squash. In a skillet, melt butter in the flour, stirring constantly. Cook about 2 minutes. Gradually stir in broth and cook, stirring, until sauce is slightly thickened. Add the first ingredients. Stir in puree. Heat. Pour into a thermos. Serve in mugs and sprinkle with bacon. Serves 8.

BARBEQUED CHICKEN

2 chickens, cut in half
¼ C. olive oil
¼ C. onions, chopped
½ C. water
¼ C. wine vinegar
½ t. paprika

¼ C. lemon juice
2 T. brown sugar
1 C. catsup
½ tsp. chili powder
½ salt
½ pepper
1 ½ T. Worcestershire sauce

Saute the onions in the oil until soft. Add all the rest of the ingredients, except the chicken, and simmer for 20 minutes. Cool. Pour over the chicken and refrigerate for 24 hours. Cook over a grill, basting frequently with the sauce.

TENDER PORK RIBS

1 pkg. country style pork ribs   Garlic salt
1 large bottle Italian dressing   Barbeque sauce

The morning before the day you will serve them, rub the ribs with the garlic salt. Marinate the ribs in the Italian dressing and wrap in foil. Refrigerate. Before going to bed, set the oven to 200 degrees F. and place ribs in the oven. Cook all night. As soon as your get up in the morning, take the ribs out of the oven. When you are ready to grill, baste the ribs with barbeque sauce and cook for 30 minutes.

POTATO SALAD WITH ARTICHOKE HEARTS

8 new potatoes   ¼ C. parsley, chopped
1 can bouillon   ½ tsp. salt
1 red onion, chopped   ½ tsp. pepper
12 cherry tomatoes   ½ small green pepper, chopped
1-4 oz. can artichoke hearts,   1 C. mayonnaise
    drained and sliced

Bake the new potatoes and cool. Peel and slice them. Marinate them in the bouillon for 1 hour. Add all the other ingredients, except mayonnaise and potatoes, in a bowl. Just before serving, drain the potatoes and mix with the rest of the ingredients. Add the mayonnaise. Serves 8.

BAKE BEANS IN MAPLE SYRUP

2-16 oz. cans baked beans
¼ C. pure maple syrup
3 T. catsup

½ tsp. A-1 steak sauce
½ tsp. Worcestershire sauce
½ tsp. dry mustard
6 slices bacon

Combine all the ingredients, except the bacon and mix well. Place in a one-quart baking dish. Place the bacon on top. You can cook this on the grill for 30 minutes. If you cook this in an oven, preheat to 350 degrees F. for 30 minutes. Serves 6 to 8.

ICED BROWNIES

1 stick butter
2 squares unsweetened chocolate
1 C. sugar
1 C. pecans, chopped

½ C. flour
1 tsp. baking powder
1 tsp. vanilla
2 eggs, beat

Melt the butter and chocolate in top of a double boiler. Stir well and remove from the heat. Add the sugar, pecans, flour, baking powder and vanilla. Mix well. Add the eggs and mix again. Pour into an 8-inch square glass pan. Place in a preheated oven at 350 degrees F. for 30 to 45 minutes. Cool well before icing.

Icing

8 oz. semisweet chocolate

1 C. heavy cream

Melt the chocolate in the cream in a double boiler, whisking until smooth. Pour over the brownies.

NOTES

COCKTAIL PARTY

OPEN BAR

STUFFED CHERRY TOMATOES
ROASTED PEPPER CHEESECAKE
SPINACH DIP IN A BREAD BOWL

BOILED SHRIMP WITH RED SAUCE
SLICE HAM AND TURKEY

HOMEMADE MUSTARD
CRANBERRY CHUTNEY

HARD ROLLS CUT IN HALF

CREAM PUFFS   APRICOT COOKIES
FRUIT AND CHEESES

"EAT BREAD AT PLEASURE.
DRINK WINE BY MEASURE."
RANDLE CATGRAVE

129

STUFFED CHERRY TOMATOES

Hollow out the tomatoes. Rinse and turn the tomatoes upside down to drain on a paper towel.

Fillings:

Guacamole

Roquefort cheese mixed with cognac and butter.

Smoked salmon mixed with cream cheese, Worcestershire sauce and chives.

Cream cheese mixed with chopped basil, Tabasco sauce, salt and pepper.

Place one or more of the fillings in the hollowed out tomatoes. Place on a platter and chill.

SPINACH DIP IN A BREAD BOWL

1 large round loaf of sourdough
 French bread
½ C. mayonnaise

4 C. yogurt
2-10 oz. packages frozen chopped
 spinach, thawed and squeezed dry
2 pkg. of dry onion soup mix

Mix together the yogurt, spinach, mayonnaise and soup mix. Cover and chill for at least 4 hours. Hollow out the bread. Fill the bowl with the spinach dip. Serve the dip with the bread pieces. Makes 20 servings.

ROASTED PEPPER CHEESECAKE

2 T. dry breadcrumbs, unseasoned
1-15 oz. ricotta cheese
1-8 oz. cream cheese, softened
1 egg

1/3 C. graded fresh Parmesan
   cheese
½ tsp. salt
¼ tsp. pepper

Grease 2 spring form pans. Sprinkle breadcrumbs evenly over the bottoms of the pans. With a mixer, beat the ricotta and cream cheese until smooth. Add the egg, Parmesan cheese, salt and pepper. Beat until well blended. Place ¾ cup of the mixture over the bread crumbs.

Roasted Pepper Pesto:

1 C. fresh basil leaves
¼ C. graded Parmesan cheese
2 T. pine nuts, toasted

1 T. olive oil
¼ tsp. salt
¼ tsp. pepper
2 lbs. red bell peppers

Roast and peel the bell peppers. Place all the ingredients in a food processor and mix until smooth. Spread ½ cup mixture over the cheese mixture in both pans. Add the ¾ cup cheese mixture on top. Bake in a preheated 325 degrees F. oven for 45 minutes.

Topping:

1 tsp. flour
¼ C. pepper pesto

1- 8 oz. carton sour cream

Combine the pepper pesto, flour and sour cream in a bowl. Stir well. Spread over both pans. Bake for 10 minutes more. Cool. Remove from pans, cover and chill. Cut each cheesecake in 12 pie wedges. Serve with French bread baguettes. Serves 24.

RED SAUCE FOR SHRIMP

½ C. chili sauce   1 T. lemon juice
½ C. ketchup   2 tsp. horseradish

Mix all the ingredients until smooth. Makes 1 cup.

HOMEMADE MUSTARD SAUCE

½ C. sugar   1 C. milk
¼ C. + 1 T. dry mustard   1 egg yolk
½ tsp. salt   ½ C. vinegar
2 T. flour

In a saucepan, mix the first 4 ingredients. Add the remaining ingredients and
cook over medium heat stirring constantly until thick and bubbly. Refrigerate
until ready to serve. Makes 1¾ cups.

CRANBERRY CHUTNEY

4 C. cranberries, chopped   1 C. cider vinegar
2 C. brown sugar   ½ C. almonds, chopped
1 C. onion, chopped   3/4 C. green pepper, chopped
1 ½ C. golden raisins   ¼ C. ginger, chopped
                                    1 clove garlic, smashed

In a large saucepan, combine all the ingredients. Bring to a boil, reduce the
heat and simmer 15 minutes. Stir occasionally. Chill. Makes 4 ½ cups.

CREAM PUFFS

Pastry:

1 C. water
¼ C. butter
¼ tsp. salt

1 C. flour
4 eggs

Heat the water to boiling. Add the butter and salt. Stir in the flour. Cook to the consistency of mashed potatoes. Add one egg at a time, beating well after each egg. On a greased cookie sheet, drop 1 tablespoon of the pastry mixture 2 inches apart. Bake in a preheated 400 degrees F. oven for 20 to 25 minutes. Cool.

Filling:

2 T. flour
¾ C. sugar

4 eggs, beaten
4 C. scalded milk
2 tsp. vanilla extract

Mix the flour with the sugar. In a double boiler, add the eggs, flour and sugar. Pour the hot milk slowly over the mixture and mix well. Add the vanilla. Cook over medium heat, do not boil, until it thickens. Cool. Cut puffs in half and fill with custard. Makes 24 puffs.

APRICOT COOKIES

1 C. dried apricots
1 C. Eagle Brand condensed milk
1 T. sugar

2 T. lemon juice
1 T. flour
2 C. pecans, chopped

Place apricots in a food processor and chop. You should have 1 cup after you chop them. Mix all ingredients together and mix well. The mixture will be thin. Drop on a greased cookie sheet in bit-size pieces. Bake in a preheated 300 degrees F. oven for 20 minutes. Makes 6 dozen.

NOTES

THANKSGIVING

CRANBERRY FROST   CAPE CODDER

SPINACH PASTRY

TURKEY AND GRAVY
SQUASH DRESSING

CRANBERRY AND ALMOND SAUCE
MINCEMEAT SALAD

BOURBON SWEET POTATOES
GREEN BEANS WITH MUSHROOMS

CROISSANTS

PUMPKIN PIE
CHOCOLATE CAKE WITH
RASPBERRY SAUCE

LET US GIVE THANKS.

CRANBERRY FROST

1 can frozen cranberry juice, thawed

1 can frozen apple juice, thawed
5 cans chopped ice

Put all ingredients in a blender and blend until smooth. You can freeze before hand. Let it soften enough to scoop into glasses. Serves 6 to 8.

CAPE CODDER

8 oz. vodka
32 oz. cranberry juice

Juice of 2 limes
Chilled club soda

Shake the first 3 ingredients and pour into chilled glasses with ice. Add the club soda. Serves 8.

SPINACH PASTRY

2 –10 oz. frozen chopped spinach,
    thawed
3 T. oleo
1 onion, chopped
12 green onions, chopped

1 egg, beaten
1/3 lb. feta cheese
1 lb. pkg. filo dough
1 C. butter, melted

Saute the onions in the oleo. Add spinach and cook until the liquid evaporates. Cool. Add the egg and feta cheese. Place the filo sheet on a board. Brush the sheet with the melted butter. Cut crosswise into 3 pieces. Place 1 teaspoon of filling at the short end of pastry. Fold lengthwise in fourths to make a long thin strip. Starting with the spinach end, fold over and over down the strip until the spinach is completely encased in a small packet about 1-inch square. Repeat with the next sheet. Place on ungreased cookie sheet. Brush tops with additional butter. Preheat oven to 350 degrees F. and cook for 20 to 25 minutes. These can be frozen and thawed before reheating. Makes 6-7 dozen.

TURKEY AND GRAVY

12 to 14 lb. turkey   Salt and pepper
1 stick butter, melted   2 C. water

Remove the paper bag found in the cavity of the turkey. Place the giblet, liver, neck and heart in a pan on the stove with enough water to cover them. Bring to a boil and reduce heat to low. Cook, uncovered, for 2 hours. Set aside, until ready to make the gravy. Wash the turkey inside and out with cool running water. Pat dry. Rub the cavity with the butter and salt and pepper. Rub the turkey all over with the butter, salt and pepper. Place in a roasting pan and pour the water in the pan. Place a shield of tin foil over the turkey. Place in a preheated oven at 350 degrees F. for 2 to 2 ½ hours. After 2 hours, remove the foil and cook 30 more minutes. Place a meat thermometer in the thigh. When it is done, the thermometer will register 175 to 180 degrees F.

Gravy:

Liquid from cooked giblets and pan   1/3 C. flour
  juices from the turkey, should measure 1/3 C. cold water
  4 cups liquid   Cooked giblets, liver and heart,
Salt and pepper to taste   chopped
4 hard boiled eggs, cut in half and   Neck, meat peeled off
  sliced

Place the liquid in a pan and bring to a boil. Mix the flour and water in a cup and stir well with a fork until you make a smooth paste. Slowly pour and stir the paste, a little at a time, to the liquid boiling in the pan. Stir until the gravy becomes as thick as you like. Add the remaining ingredients. Makes about 4 cups.

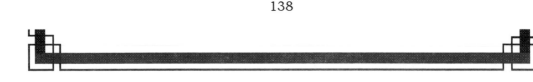

SQUASH DRESSING

1 C. corn meal
½ C. flour
1 T. baking powder
1 tsp. salt

1 T. sugar
1 tsp. baking soda
1 ½ T. oil
1 egg, beaten
1 C. buttermilk

Add all the ingredients in the order given. Mix will. Pour into a pie pan and bake in a preheated oven at 375 degrees for 30 minutes or until golden. Cool. Crumble in a large bowl.

Squash Mixture:

1 acorn squash
4 T. butter
12 slices stale bread, ends trimmed
3 celery stalks
1 onion, chopped
½ C. raisins
2 red apples, peeled and chopped

Salt and pepper to taste
½ C. pecans
2 eggs, beaten
2 ¾ C. chicken broth
1 ½ tsp. thyme
1 T. sage

Slice the squash in half and dot with 1 tablespoon butter. Bake in a preheated oven at 350 degrees F. for 40 minutes. Cool. Remove skin and chop up. Crumble the bread in the corn bread mixture. In a skillet, sauté the celery and onions in the 3 tablespoons butter until tender. Add to the cornbread mixture. Add the remaining ingredients. Mix well. Place in a buttered casserole dish. Bake in a preheated oven at 350 degrees F. for 45 minutes or until bubbly. This is better if mixed the day before, but do not add the eggs or broth. Serves 12.

CRANBERRY AND ALMOND SAUCE

1 lb. cranberries, finely chopped
2 C. water
1 cinnamon stick

3 slices of a lemon
2 C. sugar
15 blanched almonds

In a saucepan add the water, cinnamon and lemon and boil. Add the cranberries and boil gently for 15 minutes, covered. Stir in the sugar and cook for 5 minutes. Remove the lemon and cinnamon stick. Add the blanched almonds and stir. Refrigerate for several hours. This can be made several days before. Serves 6 to 8.

MINCEMEAT SALAD

2-3 oz. pkg. orange-flavored gelatin
1 ½ C. water
2 C. mincemeat
7 maraschino cherries

½ C. pecans
½ C. sour cream
3 tsp. maraschino cherry juice
2 T. pecans, chopped

Bring the water to a boil, and add the gelatin in a large bowl. Stirring until gelatin is dissolved. Chill until softly set. Fold in mincemeat and pecans in the gelatin. Spoon into oiled individual molds. Chill until firm. Combine the sour cream and cherry juice and mix well. Unmold the gelatin on a leaf of lettuce. Put a spoon full of the sour cream on top of each salad. Add the cherries and pecans on top of the sour cream. Serves 7.

BOURBON SWEET POTATOES

4 lb. yams, peeled and chopped
  in 1 ¼ -inch chunks
1 stick butter

1 C. brown sugar
½ C. frozen orange juice concentrate
1/3 C. bourbon

Butter the bottom and sides of a baking dish. Add the chopped yams to the
dish. Melt the butter in an iron skillet and add the brown sugar. Stir over
medium heat until bubbly. Remove from the heat. Stir in the concentrate until
it melts. Add the bourbon. Pour the sauce over the yams. Cover the dish
tightly with foil. Bake in a preheat oven at 350 degrees F. for 45 minutes and
then remove the foil and bake for 30 more minutes. Serves 8.

GREEN BEANS AND MUSHROOMS

1 lb. green beans
1 T. olive oil

8 oz. mushrooms, sliced
1 T. onions, minced
Salt and pepper

Break both ends off the green beans and snap in half. Steam the green beans
until tender, 10 to 15 minutes. In a skillet add the olive oil and heat. Add the
mushrooms and onions and cook until tender, about 3 to 5 minutes. Add the
green beans, salt and pepper and toss. Serves 4.

CROISSANTS

2 pkg. dry yeast
1 C. warm water
4 C. flour
¾ C. evaporated milk
1 egg, beaten

½ C. sugar
¼ C. butter, melted
2 tsp. salt
1 C. chilled butter, chopped
1 egg beaten with 1 T. water

Dissolve the yeast in the warm water in a large bowl. Add 1 cup of flour, milk, egg, sugar, melted butter and salt. Beat until smooth. Add the chopped chilled butter to the 3 cups flour in another bowl and mix well. Add to the smooth batter and blend well. Cover with plastic wrap that has been sprayed with Pam, and refrigerate for 4 hours and up to 4 days. When ready to make the croissants, remove dough and make into a ball. Knead briefly and divide dough into 4 parts. On a floured surface roll each part into a circle about 16 inches in diameter. Cut 8 pie-shaped wedges with a knife and roll loosely from edge to point. Place on an ungreased cookie sheet. Cover and let rise at room temperature. When doubled, brush with egg beaten with water. Bake in preheated oven at 400 degrees F. for 12 to 15 minutes. Makes 32 rolls.

PUMPKIN PIE

1- 8-inch pastry shell
2 large egg yolks
1 egg white, room temperature
½ C. sugar
½ C. pumpkin
¼ C. butter, melted
½ tsp. cinnamon

¼ tsp. nutmeg
¼ tsp. salt
½ tsp. lemon extract
½ tsp. vanilla extract
1/3 C.+ 2 T. scalding hot milk
1/3 C.+ 2 T. scalding hot heavy
  cream
Whipping cream, whipped

In a large bowl, beat egg yolks and gradually add sugar. Beat. Add all the ingredients, except the egg white and whipping cream. Beat well. Cool. Beat the egg white until it forms a stiff peak. Fold into pumpkin mixture. Pour into pie shell. Bake in a preheated oven at 400 degrees F. for 10 minutes. Reduce heat to 350 degrees F. and bake 25 to 30 minutes. Serve with a spoonful of the whipping cream on each slice. Serves 6.

CHOCOLATE CAKE WITH RASPBERRY SAUCE

¾ C. margarine, room temperature
1 ¼ C. sugar
4 eggs, beaten
1 tsp. vanilla

1 ½ C. flour
½ C. unsweetened cocoa powder
1 ¼ tsp. baking soda
½ tsp. salt
½ C. milk

Grease and flour 2-8-inch round cake pans. In a large bowl, beat the margarine and sugar 7 minutes, until light and fluffy. Beat in eggs and vanilla. Mix well. Add flour, cocoa, soda and salt in a bowl. Add to sugar mixture slowly, alternating with the milk. Mix well. Pour into cake pans. Bake in a preheated oven at 350 degrees F. for 25 to 35 minutes. Cool on wire racks for 5 minutes. Remove from pans. Cool completely before adding the frosting.

Frosting:
½ C. sugar
¼ C. water
2 T. corn syrup
4 oz. unsweetened chocolate, chopped

3 T. unsalted butter, melted
2 C. confectioners' sugar, shifted
2 T. very hot water
1 tsp. vanilla

In a saucepan, combine the sugar, water and corn syrup. Cover and bring to a slow boil. When sugar is completely dissolved, simmer about 3 minutes. Remove from heat and add the chocolate. Stir continuously with a metal spoon until the chocolate is dissolved. Beat the butter into the mixture and add the confectioners' sugar alternately with the hot water. Blend in the vanilla and beat until smooth and shiny. Ice the cake as soon as it is ready.

Raspberry sauce:
2-10oz. pkg. frozen raspberries in
    syrup, thawed
¼ C. sugar

3 T. Grand Marnier liqueur
1-10oz. pkg. frozen raspberries,
    thawed and drained

Drain 2 packages raspberries and discard juice of one package. Save juice of other package. Puree fruit, juice, sugar and liqueur in blender. Strain to remove seeds. Add the raspberries. Chill. Drizzle the sauce over each slice before serving.

NOTES

BUFFET PARTY

TEA PUNCH   WHITE WINE SPRITZER
FRUIT SALSA WITH CHIPS
CHILI CHEESE CAKE   SALMON SPREAD

PRIME RIB WITH HORSERADISH CREAM
CHICKEN JERUSALEM

WONDER SALAD   VEGETABLE PASTA SALAD
HEARTS OF PALM SALAD

SPINACH AND ARTICHOKE CASSEROLE
WILD RICE STRING BEANS WITH DILL VINAIGRETTE

POTATO ROLLS

LEMON TASSIES   RUM BALLS
CHOCOLATE PECAN SQUARES

"NOTHING IS TOO SMALL TO KNOW, AND
NOTHING TOO BIG TO ATTEMPT."
WILLIAM BON HORNE

145

TEA PUNCH

4 C. tea
4 C. sugar
1-12 oz. frozen orange juice, thawed
1-12 oz. frozen lemonade, thawed

1-46 oz. can pineapple juice
12 C. water
3 bottles ginger ale

Dissolve the sugar in the tea. Add the rest of the ingredients to the tea. Pour into a punch bowl with ice. Make 40 punch cup servings.

WHITE WINE SPRITZER

3 oz. club soda

Chilled white wine

Pour wine into a wine glass with ice. Fill with the club soda and stir gently.

FRUIT SALSA

2 stacks celery, chopped
4 scallions, chopped
1 green pepper, chopped
1 pear, chopped

1 apple, chopped
2 pints strawberries, chopped
2 T. lemon juice
½ C. hot sauce
2 T. salad oil

Mix first 6 ingredients in a bowl. Mix well. Add rest of ingredients. Serve with tortilla chips. Makes about 36 servings.

CHILE CHEESECAKE

Pat Snyder, Dallas, TX.

1 C. crushed tortilla chips
3 T. melted butter
2- 8 oz. softened cream cheese
2 eggs, beaten
1 fresh jalapeno pepper, cored, seeded, and diced
1-4 oz. can diced green chilies

4 oz. shredded Colby cheese
4 oz. shredded Monterey Jack cheese
½ C. sour cream
Chopped tomatoes
Chopped green onions
Diced black olives
Slice avocados

Mix the chips and butter and press into bottom of 9-inch springform pan. Preheat oven to 325 degrees F. and bake 15 minutes. Leave the oven on. Mix the cream cheese and eggs. Add the cheeses, green chiles, and jalapeno. Pour into the crust and bake 30 minutes. Remove from oven and cool 5 minutes. Remove from the pan. Spread the sour cream over the top and add the rest of the ingredients. Serve with tortilla chips. Serves 10 to 12.

SALMON SPREAD

1 can salmon, drained
1-8 oz. pkg. cream cheese, softened
1 T. green onion dip mix
1 T. lemon juice
1 tsp. Worcestershire sauce

1 clove garlic, crushed
¼ C. parsley, finely chopped
1 T. green onion, finely chopped
¼ tsp. pepper
½ tsp. salt
Pecans, chopped finely

Mix all the ingredients in a food processor, except salmon and pecans. Add salmon and mix well. Line a bowl with plastic wrap, and add the salmon shaped in a ball. Refrigerate until firm. Can be refrigerated for 2 days. Roll the ball in the pecans pieces. Place on a platter with crackers or melba toast. Serves 8 to 10.

PRIME RIB WITH HORSERADISH CREAM

Joyce Lambert, Fort Stockton, TX.

1 rib roast-allow ¾ lb. per person   Salt and pepper

Cut meat off the bone then tie meat to the bone before cooking to make serving easier. Salt and pepper the roast at this time. Have meat at room temperature before cooking. Any time from three to thirteen hours before serving, preheat oven to 375 degrees F. Bake the roast, fat side up, uncovered. Cook 1 hour for rare, 1 ½ hours for medium. After the time, turn the oven off, leaving roast in the oven. DO NOT OPEN THE OVEN DOOR! Forty-five minutes before serving turn the oven to 300 degrees.

Horseradish Cream:

1 ½ C. sour cream   1 tsp. Dijon mustard
¼ C. horseradish   ½ tsp. salt

Mix all the ingredients with a fork. Cover and refrigerate. It will keep for 2 days.

CHICKEN JERUSALEM

Carol Adams, Fort Stockton, TX.

8 boneless chicken breast, skinned
Salt and pepper to taste
½ stick of butter
2 cans mushroom caps
1 can artichoke hearts

1/3 C. sherry or white wine
1 T. lemon juice
1 C. half and half
1½ T. chives
1 C. sour cream

Salt and pepper the chicken breast. Brown the chicken breast in the butter. Add the mushrooms, artichoke hearts, sherry and lemon juice. Cook awhile and then stir in the rest of the ingredients. Place in a casserole dish and bake in a preheated 350 degrees F. oven for 1 hour.

HEARTS OF PALM SALAD

3 heads Boston lettuce
3- 14 oz. cans hearts of palm, drained

2 avocados, sliced

Tear lettuce into bite size pieces and place in a salad bowl. Add the other two ingredients. Add the dressing. Serves 12 to 14.

Dressing:

4 T. olive oil
6 T. vegetable oil
2 T. lemon juice

1 tsp. marjoram
½ tsp. tarragon
½ tsp. salt and pepper

Mix well and pour over the salad. Can be refrigerated until needed.

WONDER SALAD

Sue Walker, Lubbock, TX.

1 can LeSueus peas
1 can French-style green beans
1 can LaChoy fancy Chinese vegetables
1 can LaChoy bamboo shoots
1 can LaChoy water chestnuts, sliced

3 small onions, sliced thin
1 ½ C. diced celery
¾ C. white wine vinegar or Tarragon
    vinegar
2/3 C. sugar

Drain all the vegetables. Add the vinegar and sugar. Salt and pepper to taste. The longer it sits, the better it is.

VEGETABLE PASTA SALAD

4 C. cooked rotini
1 C. broccoli florets
1 C. cherry tomatoes, halved
2 carrots, sliced
1 bunch green onions, sliced
1/3 C. ripe olives, sliced

¼ C. Parmesan cheese, grated
2 T. fresh basil, chopped
2 T. fresh parsley, chopped
¼ C. sour cream
¼ C. buttermilk
¼ C. ranch dressing

Combine first 9 ingredients. Mix well. In another bowl, add the rest of the ingredients and mix well. Pour over the salad. Toss well and refrigerate. Serves 6 to 8.

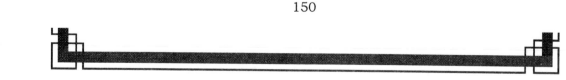

BAKED WILD RICE

1 C. wild rice, uncooked
1 ½ C. brown rice, uncooked
1 ½ T. butter
1 can condensed beef broth
3 C. water
3 T. butter
Salt to taste

1 can sliced mushrooms
2 carrots, peeled and finely chopped
1 bunch green onions, sliced
1 can sliced water chestnuts, drained
¼ C. dry white vermouth
2 T. cold butter, cut in pieces

In a bowl, add the wild rice. Add enough water to cover. Cover and let stand at least 8 hours. Drain. Add the brown rice, 1 ½ tablespoons butter, broth and water in a saucepan. Bring to a boil, cover and reduce heat and simmer 45 minutes. Make sure rice is tender. Melt the 3 tablespoons butter in a skillet and add the mushrooms, carrots, green onions and water chestnuts. Cook for 3 minutes stirring often. Add salt. Mix the vegetables with the rice. Place in a greased casserole dish. Drizzle with the vermouth and dot with the 2 tablespoons butter. Bake in a preheated 350 degrees F. oven for 40 minutes. Serves 12.

STRING BEANS WITH DILL VINAIGRETTE

5 lb. fresh string beans, ends removed

Bring 4 quarts of water to a boil. Add the green beans and cook for 6 minutes. Drain and place in a shallow dish.

Dill Vinaigrette:

½ C. white wine vinegar
2 T. Dijon mustard
1 garlic clove, crushed

1/3 C. fresh dill, chopped
2 C. olive oil
½ tsp. salt
¼ tsp. pepper

Whisk all the ingredients together and pour over the warm beans. Serves 24.

SPINACH AND ARTICHOKE CASSEROLE

2-10 oz. pkg. frozen chopped spinach,
 cooked and drained
1-8 oz. cream cheese, softened
¼ C. butter, melted

Salt and pepper to taste
½ lb. artichoke hearts
¼ c. butter, melted
1 C. seasoned bread crumbs

Combine spinach, cream cheese, butter, salt and pepper. Mix well. Place in a greased 1-qt. casserole dish and arrange artichoke hearts on top. Mix breadcrumbs with the butter. Spread over the top. Bake in a preheated 350 degrees F. oven for 20 to 30 minutes. Serves 6.

POTATO ROLLS

1 ½ C. buttermilk
2/3 C. water
¼ C. sugar
2 T. butter

1 ½ tsp. salt
¾ C. instant mashed potato flakes
½ C. green onion, thinly sliced
4 ½ C. flour
2 pkg. active dry yeast

In a saucepan, mix buttermilk, water, sugar, butter and salt. Bring to a boil. Remove from heat. Stir in the potato flakes. Let this stand for 5 minutes. Stir in the green onion. In a large bowl, add 1½ cups flour and the yeast. Mix well. Add the potato mixture and beat with an electric mixer on medium speed for 30 seconds, scraping the bowl constantly. Beat on high speed for 3 minutes. Using a wooden spoon, add the remaining flour. On a floured surface, knead dough 8 minutes. Shape in a ball. Place in a greased bowl, cover and let rise in a warm place for 1 hour. The dough needs to double. Punch the dough down. Place on a floured surface and divide in half. Cover and let rest for 10 minutes. Grease 2 large baking sheets. Divide each half of dough into 12 pieces. Shape into balls. Place on the baking sheets so the balls do not touch. Cover. Let rise for 30 minutes. Bake in preheated 375 degrees F. oven for 15 minutes. Cool on a wire rack. Makes 24 rolls.

LEMON TASSIES

Crust:

1 ¼ C. flour	½ C. cold butter
1/3 C. sugar	1 egg yolk, beaten
2 tsp. lemon peel, grated	2 T. cold water

Add the flour, sugar and lemon peel in a bowl. Mix. Cut the butter in the flour mixture until crumbly. In a separate bowl, mix the egg yolk and cold water. Add to the flour mixture and mix. Knead the dough, until a ball forms. Cover and chill for 1 hour. Divide the dough into 36 balls. Press the balls in a small ungreased muffin pans. Bake in a preheated 375 degrees F. oven for 8 to 10 minutes. Cool and remove.

Filling:

2/3 C. sugar	¼ C. water
1 T. cornstarch	2 T. butter
2 tsp. lemon peel, grated	3 egg yolks, beaten
½ C. fresh lemon juice	Powdered sugar

Stir together in a pan the sugar and cornstarch. Add the grated lemon peel, lemon juice, water and butter. Cook over medium heat till thick. Stir constantly. Add the yolks. Stir to bring to a boil. Reduce heat and cook for 2 minutes more. Spoon in the crust. Cover with plastic wrap and refrigerate until ready to serve. Dust with powdered sugar before serving. Makes 36 tassies.

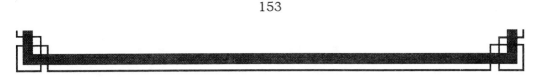

RUM BALLS

1-9 oz. pkg. Nabisco chocolate wafer
   cookies
½ C. powdered sugar
1 C. macadamia nuts, chopped
½ T. instant coffee granules

1/3 C. dark rum
3 T. dark corn syrup
2 oz. semisweet chocolate, melted
Powdered sugar

In a food processor, pulverize the cookies to make about 2 cups crumbs. Place in a large bowl. Chop the macadamia nuts in the food processor with the powdered sugar. Add to the chopped cookies. Dissolve the coffee in the rum. Add the syrup, chocolate and rum into the cookie crumbs. Pinch off pieces of dough and roll into balls. You should have 5dozen balls. Place on wax paper and let stand about 15 minutes. Dust with the powdered sugar. Store tightly covered for up to 2 days or freeze up to 2 weeks.

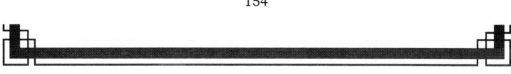

CHOCOLATE PECAN SQUARES

Crust:

¾ C. pecans, finely chopped
3 T. flour

3 T. sugar
3 T. butter, softened

Combine all ingredients in a bowl and mix. Press over bottom of an ungreased 9-inch square pan. Set aside.

Filling:

½ C. butter
1 C. sugar
3 eggs
2 squares unsweetened chocolate, melted

1 tsp. vanilla
1/3 C. flour
½ tsp. baking powder
¼ tsp. salt

Place all ingredients in a large bowl. Beat with an electric mixer at low speed until smooth. Pour over the crust. Bake in a preheated 325 degrees F. oven for 35 to 40 minutes.

Glaze:

4 oz. semi-sweet chocolate
3 T. butter

1 ¼ C. powder sugar
3 T. hot water
Chopped pecans

Melt the chocolate and butter over low heat, stirring constantly. Remove from the heat and add the sugar and water. Stir in more water if needed to drizzle over the cake. Sprinkle top with chopped nuts. When the glaze is set, cut into 1-inch squares. Makes 36 squares.

NOTES

CHRISTMAS MORNING BREAKFAST

WASSAIL

HOT PINEAPPLE AND WINE PUNCH

EGG AND SAUSAGE BAKE

BAKED APPLES

BUTTERSCOTCH BREAKFAST ROLLS

IT IS NOT HE WHO HAS LITTLE, BUT WHO
WANTS MORE IS POOR.

WASSAIL

2 C. water
2 C. sugar
1 tsp. ginger
2 sticks cinnamon
10 whole cloves

1 qt. apple cider
2/3 C. fresh lemon juice
3 ½ C. fresh orange juice
1 C. cranberry juice
3 C. strong tea

Make a syrup of the first 5 ingredients. Set out overnight. Remove the cloves and cinnamon sticks. Add the rest of the ingredients and heat over low heat. Serve warm.

HOT PINEAPPLE AND WINE PUNCH

1-46 oz. can unsweetened pineapple
    juice
½ C. sugar

¼ C. limejuice
¼ tsp. nutmeg
3 ¼ C. dry white wine

In a saucepan, place all the ingredients, except wine, and boil until sugar is dissolved. Reduce heat and add the wine. Heat until hot. Serve cinnamon sticks to the drink. Makes 2 ¼ quarts.

EGG AND SAUSAGE BAKE

1 lb. sausage, cooked
10 eggs, slightly beaten
1 C. milk
½ C. Monterey Jack cheese

½ C. feta cheese
2 T. butter, melted
2 tsp. fresh basil, chopped
2 T. flour

Mix all the ingredients together. Pour into a greased baking dish. Bake in a preheated 350 degrees F. oven for 25 minutes. This can be done in 10 custard cups. Serves 8 to 10.

BAKED APPLES

6 baking apples, cored
4 T. walnuts, chopped
4 T. raisins

1 C. water
1/3 C. honey
1 stick cinnamon
1 T. lemon juice

Peel top third of each apple and place in a shallow baking dish. Combine walnut and raisins and mix. Stuff the apples with the mixture. Combine water, honey and cinnamon stick in a saucepan. Bring to a boil and reduce heat and simmer 5 minutes. Remove from heat and stir in lemon juice. Remove the cinnamon stick. Pour over the apples. Cover and bake in a preheated 350 degrees F. oven for 45 to 50 minutes. Serves 6.

BUTTERSCOTCH BREAKFEAST ROLLS

1 pkg. frozen rolls
1 pkg. butterscotch pudding mix

¾ C. brown sugar, firmly packed
1 stick oleo
½ C. pecans, chopped

Layer frozen rolls in a greased tube cake pan. Sprinkle pudding mix and brown sugar over the rolls. Slice oleo over the rolls. Sprinkle with the pecans. Cover with a cloth and let stand overnight. Bake in a preheated 350 degrees F. oven for 25 to 30 minutes.

CHRISTMAS DAY DINNER

HOLIDAY PUNCH   EGGNOG

MUSHROOM CAPS STUFFED WITH CRAB MEAT

ROAST GOOSE WITH APRICOT DRESSING
AND GRAVY

CRANBERRY SAUCE   24 HOUR FRUIT SALAD

ORANGE RICE
BROCCOLI WITH MUSHROOM SAUCE

PHIL'S YEAST ROLLS

PUMPKIN ROLL
CHOCOLATE PECAN PIE WITH BOURBON SAUCE

"I WILL HONOR CHRISTMAS IN MY HEART
AND TRY TO KEEP IT ALL THE YEAR."
CHARLES DICKENS

HOLIDAY PUNCH

1-12 oz. can frozen orange juice, thawed
1-6 oz. can frozen lemonade, thawed

3 pints cranberry juice cocktail
1 qt. water
2 qt. ginger ale, chilled

In a large container, add all the ingredients except the ginger ale. Chill. Add the ginger ale and pour into a punch bowl filled with ice.

EGGNOG

10 whole eggs, separated
1/3 C. sugar
1 qt. heavy cream

1 pt. milk
1 fifth bourbon whiskey
4 T. rum
Nutmeg

Beat the egg whites with all but 2 tablespoons of the sugar. Beat until thick and foamy. Beat the yolks and add to the egg white mixture. Mix well. Beat the heavy cream and the 2 tablespoons of sugar until the cream doubles in size. Add the egg mixture while still beating the cream. Add the milk, whiskey and rum. Pour into a punch bowl and sprinkle with nutmeg. Chill for several hours or overnight. Serves 12.

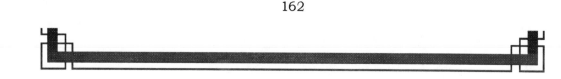

MUSHROOM CAPS STUFFED WITH CRABMEAT

12 large fresh mushrooms
1 T. butter
½ C. crab meat, drained
1/3 C. celery, chopped finely

2 T. mayonnaise
1 tsp. lemon juice
½ tsp. salt
2 T. buttered dry breadcrumbs,
    crumbled fine

Wash and trim the mushrooms. Remove the caps and set aside. Chop the stems into small pieces. Cook the mushroom stems in butter until tender. Add the crabmeat, celery, mayonnaise, lemon juice and salt. Stuff the mushroom caps and sprinkle with the crumbs. Broil in oven for 10 minutes. Serve hot.

ROAST GOOSE WITH APRICOT DRESSING

1 small goose   Salt and freshly ground pepper

Season the goose with the salt and pepper inside and out.

Dressing:
¾ C. butter   1 T. salt
¼ C. onion, chopped   ½ tsp. pepper
8 C. white bread, cubed   1 tsp. Poultry Seasoning
2 C. chicken broth   2 C. stewed apricots
                                       1 C. Brazil nuts, sliced

Saute the onion in the butter. Add the bread cubes. Toast in the oven until
very dry. Mix the bread cubes with the rest of the ingredients. Stuff the goose
with the stuffing. Close the opening with a metal skewer and place on a rack in
a shallow roasting pan. Bake in a preheated 400 degrees F. oven for 1 hour.
Turn the goose and continue to roast for another hour. Remove from oven and
pour off all the fat. Reduce the oven heat to 350 degrees F. and cook the goose
for 1 ½ to 2 hours, basting every 15 minutes with stock you will make. Remove
the dressing and place in a bowl. Serves 4.

Stock:
1 C. red wine   1 onion, chopped
1 C. consommé   8 peppercorns
1 C. water   ½ tsp. salt
Giblets from the goose   1 bay leaf
2 stalk celery, chopped   1 clove
1 carrot, chopped

Place all ingredients in a pot and boil. Reduce heat and let simmer for 45
minutes. This is the stock that you baste the goose.

Gravy:
1 T. flour   1 T. red wine
1 T. butter

Add to the remaining stock and simmer until thickened.

164

CRANBERRY SAUCE

1 ½ C. sugar
1 orange, juiced and grate the peel

½ tsp. grated ginger
4 C. cranberries
½ C. toasted pecans

In a saucepan add the orange peel, sugar and ginger. Add the juice and simmer over medium heat until sugar is dissolved. Add the cranberries and cook until they pop. Remove from heat and add the pecans. Refrigerate for several hours or overnight. Serves 6 to 8.

24 HOUR FRUIT SALAD

Carol Adams, Fort Stockton, TX.

1 C. Royal Anne cherries, pitted
1 C. pineapple cubes

1 C. marshmallows, cut in half
1 C. orange slices

Mix all ingredients in a bowl.

Dressing:

3 egg yolks, beaten
1 T. sugar

2 T. cream
½ T. lemon juice
½ pint whipping cream, whipped

Cook in a double boiler all the ingredients, except the whipped whipping cream, till thick. Cool and mix with the whipping cream. Add to the fruit and let stand 24 hours. Serves 6.

ORANGE RICE

¼ C. butter
1 onion, thinly sliced
2 tsp. curry powder
1 C. uncooked rice
1 C. orange juice

1 C. chicken broth
½ tsp. salt
½ C. raisins
1 bay leaf

Saute the onion in a saucepan with the melted butter until golden. Stir in curry and rice. Cook two minutes longer, stirring constantly. Add the rest of the ingredients and stir with a fork. Bring to a boil. Lower heat and cover. Simmer 15 to 20 minutes. Remove bay leaf and serve. Serves 6.

BROCCOLI WITH MUSHROOM SAUCE

1 bunch broccoli

1 tsp. salt

Salt the broccoli and place in a steamer. Steam until semi-tender.

Mushroom Sauce:

½ lb. mushroom caps
2 C. water, boiling
3 T. butter
4 T. flour

½ C. milk
½ tsp. salt
¼ tsp. pepper
1 T. Worcestershire sauce

Add the stems to the water. Reduce the heat and simmer for 15 minutes. In a skillet, sauté the mushroom caps in the butter for 5 minutes. Add the flour to the caps and blend well. Add the milk and 1½ cups of the mushroom stock, cooking until thickened, stirring constantly. Add the salt, pepper and Worcestershire sauce. Pour over the broccoli and serve. Makes 2 cups. Serves 4.

PHIL'S YEAST ROLLS

Phil McClure, Pagosa Springs, CO.

2 C. warm water
2 pkg. yeast
½ C. shortening
½ C. sugar

2 tsp. salt
2 eggs, beaten
6 C. flour

Dissolve yeast in the water. Add shortening, sugar, salt and eggs and mix well. Add flour. Cover and refrigerate. Let rise until doubled. Take out the amount you need. The rest will keep for a week. Flour your surface. Roll out the dough and cut out rolls with biscuit cutter. Place on a greased pan and let rise. Bake in a preheated 425 degrees F. oven for about 15 minutes or until brown. Brush with melted butter. These can be made into cinnamon rolls.

CHOCOLATE PECAN PIE WITH BOURBON SAUCE

1 unbaked 9-inch pie shell
½ C. butter
3 oz. unsweetened chocolate
4 eggs, beaten with a mixer
3 T. white corn syrup

1 ½ C. sugar
1 tsp. vanilla
¼ tsp. salt
1½ C. pecan pieces

In a double boiler, melt the butter and chocolate. Cool. Add the eggs to the corn syrup, sugar, vanilla and salt. Mix well. Stir in the pecans and chocolate mixture. Pour into the pie shell. Bake in a preheated 350 degrees F. oven for 25 to 30 minutes. Cool. Drizzle the sauce over the pie.

Bourbon Sauce:

1 C. half and half
1 T. sugar

3 egg yolks, room temperature
¼ C. pure maple syrup
¼ C. bourbon

Mix the half and half and sugar in a small saucepan, and heat over a low heat, stirring constantly. Make sure the sugar is dissolved. Remove from the heat. Beat the egg yolks with a mixer and slowly beat in the cream mixture. Return to the heat and cook until it is thick, about 2 minutes. Stir constantly. Pour in bowl and add the syrup and bourbon. Refrigerate until ready to use.

PUMPKIN CAKE ROLL

Joyce Lambert, Fort Stockton, TX.

3 eggs
1 C. sugar
2/3 C. canned pumpkin
1 tsp. lemon juice
¾ C. flour

1 tsp. baking powder
2 tsp. cinnamon
1 tsp. ginger
½ tsp. nutmeg
½ tsp. salt

Beat the 3 eggs on high for 5 minutes. Gradually beat in sugar. Stir in pumpkin and lemon juice. In a separate bowl, add the remaining ingredients. Add to the pumpkin mixture. Spread in greased and floured 15x10x1-inch jellyroll pan. Bake in a preheated 375 degrees F. oven for 15 minutes. Remove cake from oven and put on a hot, wet dishtowel that has been sprinkled with powder sugar. Roll cake and towel together. Cool 1 hour. Unroll cake, remove towel and spread with filling and reroll with filling on inside.

Filling:

6 oz. cream cheese
4 T. butter

½ tsp. vanilla
1 C. powdered sugar
1 C. chopped pecans

Beat first four ingredients until smooth. Add pecans and mix well. Spread over cake. Chill 4 to 6 hours before serving.

NOTES

NEW YEARS EVE DINNER

MOCK CHAMPAGNE   CHAMPAGNE COCKTAIL

SHRIMP PASTE   CHEESE FLAN

BEEF STROGANOFF

WALDORF SALAD

CAULIFLOWER WITH FRESH DILL SAUCE
SPINACH AND CHEESE CASSEROLE

HERB ROLLS

CHOCOLATE TURTLE CHEESECAKE OR AMARETTO BREEZE

"TO LEAVE THE OLD WITH A BURST OF SONG,
TO RECALL THE RIGHT AND FORGIVE THE WRONG;
TO FORGET THE THING THAT BLINDS YOU FAST TO
THE VAIN REGRETS OF THE YEAR THAT'S PAST."
ROBERT BREWSTER BEATTIE

MOCK CHAMPAGNE

½ C. sugar
1 C. water
1-6 oz. frozen grapefruit juice,
   thawed

1-6 oz. can frozen orange juice,
   thawed
1 bottle ginger ale, chilled
1/3 C. grenadine syrup

Combine sugar and water in a saucepan and bring to a boil. Boil for 5 minutes. Let cool. Add orange juice and grapefruit juice. Mix well and refrigerate. At serving time, add ginger ale and grenadine syrup to the sugar mixture. Pour into champagne flutes. Serves 8.

CHAMPAGNE COCKTAIL

½ C. strawberries, chopped
1 orange, peeled and chopped
½ C. fresh pineapple, chopped

3 T. sugar
6 oz. Cognac
1 bottle champagne, chilled

Mix fruit and sprinkle with sugar. Pour Cognac over the mixture. Chill for 1 hour. Divide mixture into 6 pre-chilled champagne glasses. Fill with the champagne. Serves 6.

CHEESE FLAN

½ C. milk
4 eggs, separated
½ C. butter

½ C. flour
2 C. cheddar cheese, large grated
1 large can chopped green chilies

Beat the milk, egg yolks, butter and flour until smooth. Add the cheese and mix well. Fold in the chilies. Beat egg whites until stiff and fold gently into the mixture. Pour into two 8-inch pie pans. Bake in a preheated 375 degrees F. oven for 15 minutes. If you want to freeze it before hand, do not cook it until ready to serve. Cut into small wedges and serve.

SHRIMP PASTE

4 ½ oz. canned deveined shrimp
5 T. miracle whip

2 tsp. finely minced onion
¼ tsp. salt
1/8 tsp. curry powder

Drain the shrimp and soak in ice water for 20 minutes. Mash the shrimp. Add the rest of the ingredients. Refrigerate for at least an hour. Serve with crackers or toast.

173

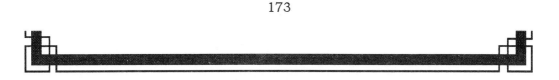

BEEF STROGANOFF

Stacy Saba, Tempe, AZ.

½ C. onion, chopped
¼ C. butter, melted
4-4 oz. cans sliced mushrooms,
   drained
3 lbs. sirloin steak, cut into ½-inch
   strips

1 can beef broth
½ C. flour
½ tsp. salt
½ tsp. pepper
½ tsp. paprika
2-8 oz. cartons sour cream
Cooked noodles

Saute onions in the butter until transparent. Stir in the mushrooms. Add beef and cook until brown. Add next 5 ingredients. Reduce heat and simmer for 10 to 12 minutes. Remove from the heat and add the sour cream. Heat until hot. Serve over the noodles. Serves 8 to 10.

WALDORF SALAD

1lb. cranberries, chopped
6 apples, peeled and chopped
4 celery stalks, chopped
1 C. walnuts, chopped

1 C. raisins
4 T. fresh lemon juice
1 C. mayonnaise
1 ½ C. sugar

Combine the first 5 ingredients. In a separate bowl, add the remaining ingredients and mix well. Pour over the fruit and mix well. Place a leaf of lettuce on 8 salad plates and add the salad. Serves 8.

CAULIFLOWER WITH FRESH DILL SAUCE

1 head cauliflower
2 T. butter
2 T. flour
½ C. milk

2 T. chopped fresh dill
1 T. chopped parsley
½ tsp. grated onion
½ tsp. salt
½ C. sour cream

Trim the cauliflower and cook in a covered pan with 1-inch of boiling salt water. Cook for 15 to 20 minutes or until tender. In a small saucepan, melt the butter over low heat. Add the flour, stirring constantly, for 1 minute. Remove from heat, and add milk. With a whisk, mix well. Return to the heat, and add all the ingredients, except the sour cream. Cook until mixture boils. Lower the heat and add the sour cream. Cook until heated throughout. Place the cauliflower in a serving dish, and pour the sauce over it. Serves 6 to 8.

SPINACH AND CHEESE CASSEROLE

4 eggs, beaten
½ tsp. salt
½ tsp. pepper
1-10 oz. pkg. frozen chopped spinach,
    thawed, and squeezed dry

1-16 oz. cottage cheese
1 bunch green onions, chopped
1 C. packed grated sharp cheddar
    cheese
¼ C. flour
3 T. fresh dill, chopped

Add all the ingredients and mix well. Pour into an 8-inch glass baking dish. Bake in a preheated 350 degrees F. oven for 45 minutes. Serves 8 to 10.

HERB DINNER ROLLS

1 pkg. dry yeast
1 T. sugar
1 C. warm water
1 C. milk, warmed
2 eggs, beaten
1 T. salt

2 T. butter
¼ C. fresh parsley, chopped fine
¼ C. fresh chives, chopped fine
6 C. flour
1 egg white
2 T. water

Mix the yeast, sugar and water and let stand for 10 minutes. In a large mixing bowl, add the milk, eggs, salt, butter, parsley, chives and 4 cups of the flour. Stir until mixed well. Add the remaining flour, a little at a time, and mix well. Place on a floured surface and knead 8 minutes. Place the dough in a greased bowl and cover with a damp cloth. Let rise in a warm spot for 1 hour. Divide the dough into 18 equal pieces and place on greased 9x13-inch baking pan. Cover with a damp cloth and let rise for 45 minutes. Mix the egg white and water in a bowl. Brush on the tops of the rolls. Bake in preheated 350 degrees F. oven for 30 minutes or until golden brown. Makes 18 rolls.

AMARETTO BREEZE

1 qt vanilla ice cream

¼ C. brandy
¼ C. amaretto

Combine all ingredients in a blender and blend until smooth. Makes 4 ½ cups.

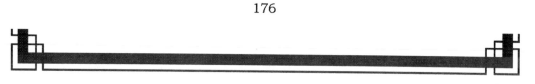

CHOCOLATE TURTLE CHEESECAKE

Crust:

1½ C. chocolate sandwich cookies,
   crumbled

3 T. butter, melted

Mix the ingredients and press into a 9-inch pie plate. Bake in preheated 350 degrees F. oven for 6 to 8 minutes.

Filling,

1-7 oz. pkg. caramels
¼ C. evaporated milk
¾ C. chopped pecans
2-3 oz. pkg. cream cheese, softened

½ C. sour cream
1 ¼ C. milk
1-3.9 oz. pkg. chocolate instant
   pudding mix
½ C. fudge topping

Place caramels and evaporated milk in a saucepan. Heat over medium-low heat stirring continually for 5 minutes. Sir in ½ cup of the pecans. Pour in the piecrust. Place in a blender, the cream cheese, sour cream and milk. Blend until smooth. Add pudding mix and blend for 30 seconds. Pour over caramel mixture. Chill until firm. Drizzle fudge topping over the cheesecake and sprinkle the remaining pecans over the top. Chill loosely covered. This can be made the day before. Serves 12.

NOTES

GREEK FEAST

POMEGRANATE DRINK   OUZO

STUFFED GRAPE LEAVES
CUCUMBER DIP WITH PITA BREAD

ROAST LAMB

GREEK SALAD

ZUCCHINI AND MUSHROOM CASSEROLE

BROILED TOMATOES

OLIVE AND FETA CHEESE BREAD

BAKLAVE   GREEK COFFEE

IT IS EASIER TO TALK THAN TO
HOLD ONE'S TONGUE.
GREEK PROVERB

POMEGRANATE DRINK

4 ripe pomegranates   ½ C. sugar
Juice of ½ lemon

Peel the pomegranates and add the seeds in a blender. Mix well. Strain through cheesecloth into a pitcher. Sir in the lemon juice and sugar. Chill. Serve over ice. Serves 4.

STUFFED GRAPE LEAVES

Filling:

2 T. olive oil	2 C. chicken broth
1 C. scallions, finely chopped	½ C. pine nuts
1 C. long-grain rice	½ C. dark raisins
1 tsp. cinnamon	½ C. fresh dill, coarsely chopped
1 tsp. salt	¼ C. parsley, finely chopped
1 bay leaf	Juice of ½ lemon
	Pepper to taste

Saute the scallions in the olive oil, about 4 to 5 minutes. Add the cinnamon and rice and stir well with a wooden spoon. Add the salt, bay leaf and broth. Bring to a boil and cook uncovered for about 8 minutes. Stir in the pine nuts and raisins and cover the pan with 2 layers of paper towels and lid and remove from the stove. This needs to set for 15 minutes. After this has set for 15 minutes, remove the bay leaf. Add the dill, parsley, lemon juice and pepper.

Grape leaves:
40 small leaves, plus extra leaves to cover a baking dish.

Trim off the stems and rinse thoroughly before using. Place in a large saucepan with water and bring to a boil. Blanch for 5 seconds. Remove and place on paper towels and blot dry. Line a large skillet with the extra leaves. Place the other leaves glossy side down and the stems toward you. Place 1 heaping teaspoon on each grape leaf. Pull the stem end over and fold in both sides. Firmly roll up the leaf towards the point of the leaf. Do the same until all leaves are done. Place in the skillet that is lined with the rest of the leaves. Do not wrap grape leaves too tightly, as rice will expand.

Liquid:

2 T. olive oil	Water
Juice of ½ of a lemon	

Mix ingredients with enough water to cover the leaves. Cover with a heavy lid and heat on medium-low heat. Bring to a boil and then reduce the heat and simmer 25 minutes. You may need to add water to cover the leaves. Remove from heat and serve. Serves 8.

CUCUMBER DIP

½ qt. yogurt
3 garlic cloves

½ C. olive oil
½ cucumber, peeled and diced in
    small pieces

Place the garlic through a garlic press, and add to the yogurt in a bowl. Add the cucumbers. Slowly mix the oil with a fork. Add a few olives on top. Chill. Serve with pita bread cut into quarters.

ROAST LAMB

8 lb. leg of lamb, butter flied
Salt and pepper
3 tsp. dried dill weed
Juice of 1 lemon
2 tsp. dried onions

2 tsp. dried celery
Paprika
2 T. olive oil
½ C. dry sauterne
½ lemon

Season the inside part of the lamb by rubbing salt, pepper, 2 teaspoons of the dill weed and lemon juice. Sprinkle with onions and celery. Roll up the lamb, fat side out, and tie with twine at the bottom. Place in a baking pan and season top and sides with salt, pepper, paprika and remaining 1 teaspoon dill weed. Rub well with olive oil. Pour the sauterne into pan. Preheat oven to 400 degrees F. and cook for 20 minutes, basting two or three times. Lower heat to 300 degrees F. and cook for 40 minutes. When the lamb is done, squeeze the ½ lemon over the top. Serves 8 to 10.

GREEK SALAD

1 head iceberg lettuce, torn into bit size
  pieces
4 tomatoes, cut into wedges

1 red onion, slice into thin rings
2 cucumbers, slice thin
1 ½ C. black calamata olives
¾ lb. feta cheese

Combine the lettuce, tomatoes, onions and cucumbers in a large salad bowl, and toss. Add the olives on top. Crumble the cheese and put on top. Chill.

Dressing:

6 T. red wine vinegar
½ C. olive oil

2 tsp. dried oregano
½ tsp. salt
Ground black pepper to taste

Combine all the ingredients into a jar or bottle with a lid. Shake well. Pour over the salad. Serves 6 to 8.

BROILED TOMATOES

8 tomatoes, ends slice off
½ C. bread crumbs, unseasoned
6 T. parsley, chopped
2 cloves garlic, mashed

2 tsp. basil
¼ C. olive oil
½ tsp. salt
½ tsp. pepper

Scoop out the meat of the tomatoes. Drain the shells of the tomatoes. Add the meat of the tomatoes to the rest of the ingredients. Stuff the shells with the mixture. Place in shallow baking dish and bake in preheated oven at 375 degrees F. for 25 minutes. Serves 8.

ZUCCHINI AND MUSHROOM CASSEROLE

1 lb. zucchini, peeled and sliced
¼ tsp. fresh dill, minced
1 clove garlic
4 T. butter
1 lb. mushroom, sliced

3 T. flour
1 C. sour cream
Salt taste
Black pepper to taste
1 C. bread croutons
¼ C. butter, melted

Put the zucchini, dill and garlic in a pan of boiling water. Cover and simmer
until zucchini is tender. Drain, reserving 3 tablespoons of liquid. Discard the
garlic. Saute mushrooms in the butter for 3 minutes, stirring occasionally. Stir
in the flour and cook for 2 minutes. Add sour cream, zucchini and the cooking
liquid, stirring constantly. Salt and pepper. Pour mixture in a 2-quart
casserole. Toss bread croutons and butter and sprinkle on top of casserole.
Place under broiler until brown. Serves 8.

OLIVE AND FETA CHEESE BREAD

1 pkg. yeast
¼ C. warm water
1 t. honey
1 C. warm milk
¼ tsp. salt

1 t. sugar
6 t. olive oil
3 ½ C. flour
¾ C. green olives, chopped
¾ C. feta cheese, cubed
1 egg yolk, beaten with 1 tsp. water

Mix the honey in the water. Sprinkle the yeast in the water. Add the milk, salt,
sugar and 4 teaspoons of olive oil. Mix. Add flour. Turn onto a floured surface
and knead for 15 minutes. Place in a greased bowl, cover and let rise 1 hour.
Remove and pat into a circle. Sprinkle with the olives and cheese. Shape into a
ball. Place on a greased baking pan and cut a circle in the center. Leave the
round of dough in place. Brush with 2 teaspoons of oil. Let rise 30 minutes.
Brush with egg yolk. Bake in a preheated oven at 375 degrees F. for 30
minutes. Serve hot.

BAKLAVA

1-17 ¼ oz. pkg. frozen phyllo pastry,
   thawed
1 ¼ C. butter, melted
1 ¼ C. coconut, lightly toasted
½ C. macadamia nuts, finely chopped
   and toasted

¾ C. pecans, finely chopped pecans
½ C. firmly packed brown sugar
1 tsp. allspice
1 C. sugar
½ C. water
¼ C. honey

Cut the phyllo in half crosswise and cut each half to fit the pan. Cover the phyllo with a slightly damp towel. Layer 10 sheets of phyllo in a 13x9x2-inch baking pan, brushing each sheet with melted butter. Combine coconut, nuts, pecans, brown sugar and allspice. Stir well. Sprinkle 1/3 of mixture over the phyllo. Top with 10 sheets of phyllo, brushing each sheet with melted butter. Repeat two more times, ending with the buttered phyllo. Cut the last layer of the phyllo into diamond shapes. Bake in a preheated oven at 350 degrees for 45 minutes until brown. Set aside and let cool. In a saucepan, add the water and bring to a boil. Add the sugar and honey. Reduce heat and simmer 5 minutes. Remove from heat and drizzle syrup over baklava. Cover and let stand at room temperature 24 hours. Make 3 dozen.

FRESH FRUIT WITH HYMETTUS HONEY

Use whatever fresh fruit is in season. Drizzle with the honey and refrigerate for at least 2 hours before serving.

GREEK COFFEE

4 coffee cups water
4 tsp. powder-fine ground coffee

4 tsp. sugar

Bring the water to a boil. Remove from the heat and sprinkle the coffee and sugar over the water. Bring to a boil again, and remove from the heat. Stir until the froth has disappeared, and return to high heat. Remove from the heat, stir again until the froth disappears and boil one more time. Divide the froth among the cups and carefully pour in the coffee to the brim. The froth will rise to the surface. Serves 4.

NOTES

ITALIAN FEAST

NON-ALCOHOLIC WINE   WINE

SPINACH BREAD WITH BASIL DIPPING OIL

SPICY MEATBALLS   LINGUINE WITH PESTO SAUCE

GRILLED PORTEGELLOS MUSHROOMS

ITALIAN PORK CHOPS

SPINACH SALAD

EGGPLANT ROLLS

TIRAMISU

ICE CREAM WITH CHERRIES IN BRANDY

THERE IS NO SUCH THING AS
A LITTLE GARLIC.

187

SPINACH BREAD

1 pkg. yeast
1 C. warm water
1 tsp. sugar
½ tsp. salt

2 T. olive oil
¼ C. salad oil
2 ¾ C. flour
½ -10 oz. pkg. frozen chopped
    spinach, thawed

Dissolve the yeast in the warm water. Mix in the sugar, salt, oils and 1½ cups of the flour. Beat together to form a sticky batter. This takes about 10 minutes. Squeeze the spinach dry with a paper towel. Add the spinach. Knead in the remaining flour until smooth. Allow the dough to rise right in the bowl, until doubled. This takes about 1 hour. Punch the dough down and let rise again. On a lightly oiled pan, 11x17-inch, press the dough out with your fingers evenly to the edges of the pan. Allow to rise 30 minutes. Brush on the topping and bake at 375 degrees F. for 30 to 35 minutes or until lightly browned. Serves 8.

Topping:

2 cloves garlic, crushed
2 T. olive oil

2 tsp. kosher salt

Mix together and brush on top of bread.

BASIL DIPPING FOR THE BREAD

2 C. olive oil
1 shallot, peeled
4 cloves garlic, peeled
¼ C. basil leaves
3 sprigs parsley

1 tsp. kosher salt
½ tsp. pepper
1 leaf sage
2 T. lemon juice
2 oz. grated Parmesan cheese
1 T. toasted pine nuts

Combine all the ingredients in a blender and blend until smooth. Serve with the bread.

SPICY MEATBALLS

1 lb. ground meat
1 tsp. grated Parmesan cheese
1 tsp. dried oregano
½ tsp. garlic salt
¼ tsp. pepper
½ tsp. dried basil
1 egg

2 T. lemon juice
¼ C. olive oil
1 clove garlic, chopped
1 red chili, seeded and chopped
½ red onion, chopped
1 ½ lbs. tomatoes, chopped
1 T. dry red wine

Mix the first 8 ingredients together. Shape into 1-inch balls. Saute the garlic, red chili and onion in the olive oil. Add the meatballs and cook until the meatballs are brown. Stir in the tomatoes and wine. Serve in a chafing dish. Serves 6.

GRILLED PORTOBELLO MUSHROOMS

2 Portobello mushrooms
2 oz. olive oil
1 oz. gorgonzola cheese

4 oz. heavy cream
¼ tsp. cayenne pepper
Handful of dry roasted walnuts

Brush the mushrooms with the olive oil. Grill on high, and then reduce to medium heat until mushrooms get soft to the touch. You can pan fry if you wish. Keep warm. Scald cream, remove from heat. Add the cheese and pepper and cook on low heat. Cook until thick. Slice the mushrooms ¼ inch thick. Place on a plate and cover with sauce and walnuts. Serves 4.

LINGUINE WITH PESTO SAUCE

1 lb. linguine, cooked

Pesto sauce:

36 basil leaves
3 cloves garlic
½ C. pine nuts
1¾ C. Romano cheese, grated

1¾ C. Parmesan, grated
7 oz. olive oil
½ tsp. salt
¼ tsp. pepper
3 T. boiling pasta water

Cook the linguine. Place basil leaves and garlic in a food processor. Mix. Gradually add the nuts, cheeses and olive oil. Add salt and pepper. Add the water to the pesto sauce and mix. Pour over pasta. Serves 4 to 6.

SPINACH SALAD

1 bunch spinach, wash and dry
1 red onion, sliced thin

2 small zucchini, sliced thin
3 hard boiled eggs, slice thin

Mix in a salad bowl. Chill until ready to serve.

Dressing:

2 raw eggs
½ tsp. Worcestershire sauce
3 T. Parmesan cheese, grated
1 ½ lemons, just the juice
1 tsp. Dijon mustard

½ C. extra virgin olive oil
1 ½ tsp. sugar
Fresh ground pepper, to taste
½ tsp. salt
6 slices bacon, cooked and
   crumbled

In a food processor combine all the ingredients, except the bacon. Blend. Add the bacon to the dressing. Pour over salad and toss. Serves 6 to 8.

ITALIAN PORK CHOPS

4 pork chops
2 tsp. dried rosemary, crushed
2 tsp. sage
3 cloves garlic, crushed

1 tsp. salt
½ tsp. pepper
½ C. dry white wine
1 C. water

In a bowl, add rosemary, sage, garlic, salt and pepper. Rub the pork chops with this mixture. In a large iron skillet, place the pork chops and water. Cook over low heat for 40 to 45 minutes. When the pork chops begin to brown, turn several times, until both sides are browned. Add wine and boil. Remove from heat and serve. Serves 4.

EGGPLANT ROLLS

2 eggplants, peeled and sliced lengthwise

3 C. bread crumbs, unseasoned	2 C. tomato sauce
1 ½ C. flour	1-15oz. ricotta cheese
2 eggs	1-8oz. mozzarella cheese, grated
¼ C. milk	¾ C. Romano cheese, grated
¾ C. olive oil	½ C. parsley, chopped

In a bowl, combine breadcrumbs and flour. Set aside. In a bowl, add milk and eggs and mix. Dip the eggplant in the milk mixture and then in the crumb mixture. Heat the oil in a skillet and fry the eggplant pieces for 1 to 2 minutes on each side. Mix the cheeses and parsley together. Spread the cheese mixture on the eggplants and roll up. Place in a baking dish and spread the tomato sauce over the top. Bake in a preheated oven at 350 degrees F. for 30 minutes. Serves 6.

TIRAMISU

2 pkgs. ladyfingers	6 eggs, separated
½ C. brewed espresso coffee, cooled	6 T. sugar
3 T. Kahlua	2 lb. Marscapone cheese
	4 T. unsweetened cocoa

Place half the ladyfingers in a 9x13-inch dish. In a small bowl, combine coffee and Kahlua. Sprinkle on the ladyfingers. Beat egg yolks and sugar with mixer until thick. Add marscapone and blend on low speed until combined. In a large bowl, beat egg whites with electric mixer until soft peaks form. Add to marscapone mixture. Pour half of the mixture on the ladyfingers. Sift 2 T. of the cocoa over the ladyfingers. Repeat. Cover with plastic and chill overnight. Serves 8.

ICE CREAM WITH CHERRIES IN BRANDY

1-16 oz. can bing cherries   ½ C. brandy
   in heavy syrup   1 ½ T. sugar

Drain the cherries, saving the syrup. Place the cherries in a bowl and pour the brandy over them. Simmer the syrup and sugar in a small saucepan until reduced by half. Allow to cool and add the syrup to the cherries. Cover and place in the refrigerator overnight. Serve over ice cream. Serves 4.

NOTES

INDEX

APPETIZERS AND SOUPS

BREAD, SWEET BREAD AND EGGS

EGGS

DESSERTS

DRINKS

Non-Alcoholic:

Alcoholic Drinks:

MAIN DISHES

SALADS AND SAUCES

VEGETABLES